Prevailing Trade Winds

Prevailing Trade Winds

Climate and Weather in Hawai'i

Edited by Marie Sanderson

 UNIVERSITY OF HAWAII PRESS, HONOLULU

© 1993 University of Hawaii Press
All rights reserved
Printed in the United States of America

98 97 96 95 94 93   5 4 3 2 1

Library of Congress Cataloging-in-Publication Data
Prevailing trade winds : climate and weather in Hawai'i / edited by
   Marie Sanderson.
     p.   cm.
   Includes bibliographical references and index.
   ISBN 0-8248-1491-6
   1. Hawaii—Climate.   I. Sanderson, Marie.
QC984.H3P74   1993   93–21595
551.69969—dc20   CIP

Cartography by Ev Wingert

University of Hawaii Press books are printed on acid-free
paper and meet the guidelines for permanence and durability
of the Council on Library Resources

Design by Kenneth Miyamoto

Contents

Figures

Tables

Preface

THIS BOOK is about the climate and weather of the Hawaiian Islands. Dictionaries define "weather" as the current state of the atmosphere, and "climate" as "average weather." The climate of a place, however, is more than the sum of various weather elements such as temperature and precipitation but involves the variability and frequency of occurrence of these phenomena. As we will see in the following pages, the study of climate also includes the examination of the exchanges of energy and moisture at the surface of the earth. We discuss the early Hawaiians' concept of climate and also attempt to show the impact of climate on human activities and the effect of human actions on climate.

The book is intended for meteorologists, geographers, biologists, ecologists, hydrologists, and others who are interested in climate and weather phenomena. We have written the book mainly for beginning college and university students, but we believe that it will be useful as well to the environmental scientist and the interested layperson. We hope that we make understandable the reasons for the loveliness of the climate of Hawai'i, truly the climate of Paradise.

CHAPTER 1

Introduction

Marie Sanderson

"THE LOVELIEST fleet of islands that lies anchored in any ocean," wrote Mark Twain of the Hawaiian Islands, and millions of tourists have shared this famous sentiment. The charm of the Islands is a result of many visible natural phenomena: the beautiful flowers, the palm trees, the lush green slopes, the high mountains, and the encircling ocean. However, for most people, the essence of Hawai'i is its year-round pleasant climate, never too hot and never too cold, with moderate humidities and air-conditioning trade winds. Although the Islands lie within the tropics, they do not suffer the usual tropical heat. Anchored as they are in the middle of the Pacific Ocean, they are naturally protected from extremes by that huge body of water.

The state of Hawai'i is composed of eight main islands with a total land area of 16,642 km² (6,425 mi²). The largest, Hawai'i (called the Big Island), has an area of 10,451 km² (4,035 mi²), more than three times the size of the state of Rhode Island and more than five times the size of Maui, the next largest. In descending order are the other islands of O'ahu, Kaua'i, Moloka'i, Lāna'i, Ni'ihau, and little Kaho'olawe with an area of only 116 km² (45 mi²). The main islands range from approximately 19° to 22° north latitude and from 154° to 160° west longitude. There are also numerous small islands and atolls. The chain of islands extends for some 2,451 km (1,523 mi) from Kure Atoll and Midway Islands in the northwest to Hawai'i in the southeast.

The Islands are relatively young geologic features on the surface of the earth. Millions of years ago, fissures opened on the ocean floor in this area of the Pacific Ocean and layer upon layer of molten rock emptied from deep inside the earth's crust. These layers of rock gradually piled up to build the mountains now known as the Hawaiian Islands. When the mountains rose above the surface of the ocean, they became susceptible to erosion by wind, rain, and waves. The topography of the Islands is a result almost entirely of their volcanic origin.

Geologically, Kaua'i is the oldest of the major islands (about 4.5–5.6 million years) while the island of Hawai'i, parts of which are 0.5 million years old, is actually still growing in the southeast. Consequently, the older islands, Kaua'i and O'ahu,

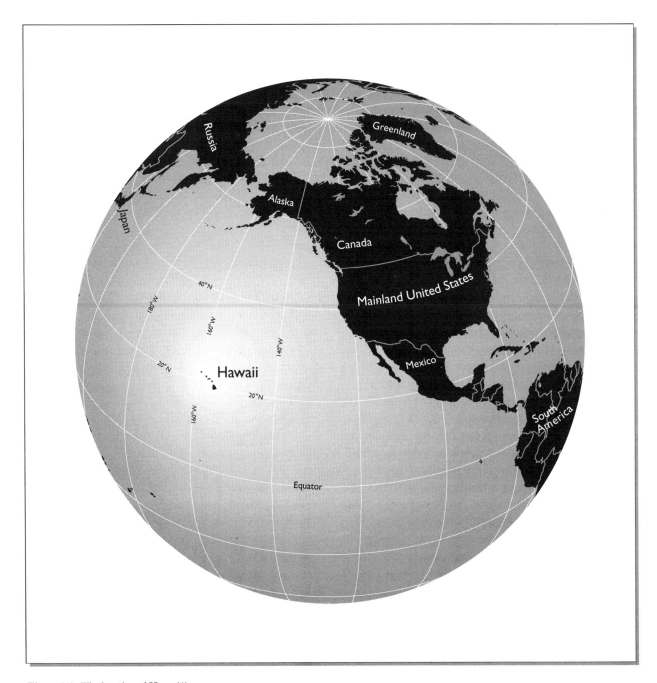

Figure 1.1 The location of Hawai'i

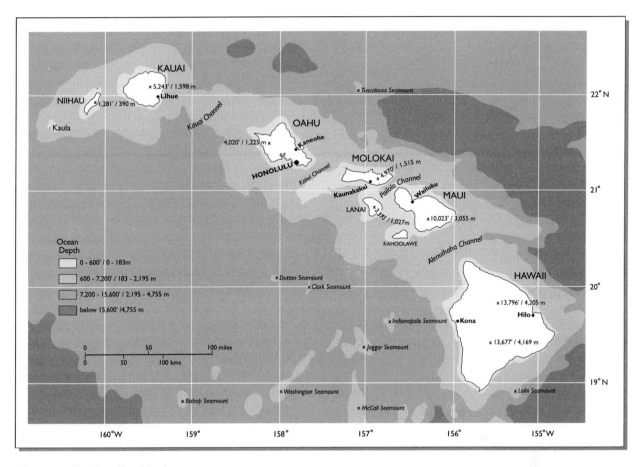

Figure 1.2 The Hawaiian Islands

situated in the northwest of the island chain, have been exposed to the atmosphere longer and are more deeply eroded than the easterly islands. Even the lowest island, Niʻihau, is a volcanic mountain rising more than 3,900 m (12,800 ft) above its base on the ocean floor. The tops of the highest mountains, Mauna Kea and Mauna Loa on the island of Hawaiʻi, are more than 9,000 m (30,000 ft) above the bottom of the ocean. The geology of the Islands is well described in *Volcanoes in the Sea* (University of Hawaii Press, 1983).

The general topography of the Hawaiian Islands is seen in Figure 1.3. Kauaʻi is almost circular, with one large mountain, whose highest peak, Kawai-kini, reaches to 1,598 m (5,243 ft). Oʻahu has two parallel mountain chains; the Koʻolau Range defines the northeast coast and the Waianae Range the southwest, with Kaʻala the highest elevation at 1,225 m (4,020 ft). Elevations in West Molokaʻi are 436 m (1,430 ft), but an old volcanic cone in the eastern part of the island reaches 1,515 m (4,970 ft). Maui has two volcanic cones—Puʻu Kukui in West Maui at 1,764 m (5,788 ft) and Haleakalā in East Maui, with a summit at 3,055 m (10,023 ft). The

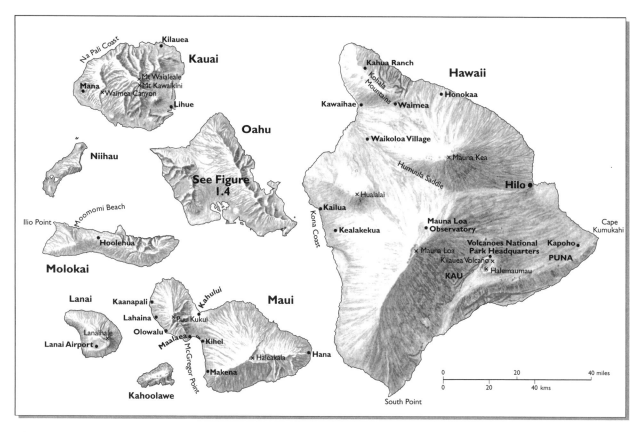

Figure 1.3 Major topographic features of the Hawaiian Islands and location of places in text

island of Hawai'i has the most interesting topography, the giant shield volcanoes of Mauna Kea and Mauna Loa having elevations respectively of 4,205 m (13,796 ft) and 4,169 m (13,679 ft). Because their summits lie above much of the earth's atmosphere, these two mountains have become important sites for observatories—astronomical observatories on Mauna Kea and an atmospheric observatory on Mauna Loa.

Relief features on the Islands are partly the result of their volcanic origins, and partly the result of erosion. For example, the largest features, such as the mountain masses of Mauna Loa or Mauna Kea, called "shield volcanoes," are geologically recent

volcanoes, built by many thin lava flows. Features of intermediate size include posterosional volcanic cones like Diamond Head, Koko Head, and the Punchbowl on O'ahu. Water erosion has carved out some deep valleys in the Islands; for instance, Waimea Canyon on Kaua'i is 850 m (2,800 ft) in depth. In places, erosion by waves has caused the edges of the islands to form sea cliffs like those on the north side of East Moloka'i, which rise to 990 m (3,250 ft) above the sea, the world's highest. The Nā Pali coast on Kaua'i is another spectacular sea cliff.

The volcanic origins of the Hawaiian Islands also greatly affect the water balance of the state. The basaltic rocks are quite permeable to water, with most of the rain that falls flowing through the rocks to the water table, with very little surface runoff. The impact of geology on the water balance will be described in more detail in a later chapter.

The geology of Hawai'i makes for interesting scenery, but it also greatly affects all aspects of the climate. The climates of the Islands are the result of their position on the earth's surface and the great ocean that surrounds them, but the topography causes great local variation. Half the area of Hawai'i lies above 600 m (2,000 ft) in elevation, and 10% lies above 2,100 m (7,000 ft). The mountains, especially the massive ones on Hawai'i and Maui, modify the effect of the ocean and lead to marked contrasts in climate between the windward and the leeward slopes. Winds are deflected in various ways by the mountains and valleys, resulting in striking differences in wind speed, cloudiness, and rainfall over very small distances.

Climatically, the Hawaiian Islands are very interesting, resembling continents in miniature, with tropical rain forests, grasslands, deserts, even tundra areas. Here we find one of the rainiest places on earth, Wai'ale'ale on the island of Kaua'i, with nearly 11,430 mm (450 in) of rain in an average year, as well as deserts with less than 250 mm (10 in). The steepest rainfall gradients recorded anywhere in the world are found here: 420 mm of rainfall per year for each kilometer (26.6 in per mile) traversed. Yet this diversity exists on islands that together have an area about one-third larger than the state of Connecticut.

The Hawaiian Islands lie in the tropics, so they do not have great seasonal differences in length of day. In Honolulu, the longest day is 13 hours 20 minutes and the shortest is 10 hours 50 minutes. Compare this to Seattle, for example, whose longest day is 16 hours and the shortest 8 hours 20 minutes. Hawai'i is located more than 3,700 km (2,300 mi) from any major continent (Figure 1.1). The surface tempera-

ture of the ocean in the vicinity of Hawai'i varies between only 22.5° and 25°C (72°–77°F) in winter and 25–27.5°C (77–81°F) in summer, with the maximum temperatures occurring in August/September and the minimum temperatures in February/March, with isotherms parallel to the island chain. Because the Islands are small, no area is far from the ocean, and thus the marine influence on the climate is felt everywhere. Even on the Big Island no area is more than 45 km (28 mi) from the ocean.

Because of this marine influence, temperatures in Hawai'i vary little from winter to summer. For example, at the Honolulu airport (21°N), the average maximum temperature for August, the hottest month, is 31.5°C (88.7°F), and the average minimum temperature is 23.4°C (74.2°F). During the coldest month, January, the average maximum temperature is 26.7°C (80.1°F) and average minimum 18.6°C (65.4°F). The difference between winter and summer, for both maximum and minimum temperature, is only about 4.5°C (8°F).

In contrast, Miami, Florida (26°N), has a more continental range of temperatures. August, the hottest month, has an average maximum temperature of 32°C (89.9°F) and a minimum of 24.2°C (75.8°F), while January, the coldest month, has an average maximum of 24.2°C (75.6°F) and a minimum of 15°C (58.7°F). The difference between average winter and summer temperatures in Miami is 8°C (14°F) for the maximum and 9°C (16°F) for the minimum temperature, about double the range for Honolulu.

Although the climate near the ocean margins of the Islands varies little from winter to summer, one need go only a few miles inland to higher elevations to notice distinct changes. When visitors arrive at the Honolulu airport, they enter a climate which varies little from season to season and where the annual mean temperature is 25°C (77°F). Only a few miles away at Niu Ridge, however, the annual temperature is 22 °C (71 °F). Much higher, at the observing station on Mauna Loa at 3,400 m (11,200 ft) on the Big Island, the average temperature for the year is only 6.7 °C (44 °F).

Observant visitors will also notice that it rains much more along the mountain slopes than along the sea shore. In Honolulu the yearly rainfall averages 560 mm (22 in), while at the head of Manoa Valley, a few miles inland at 200 m (650 ft), it is 4,013 mm (158 in). Monthly figures of temperature and precipitation from seven representative stations in the Islands are given later in the book.

The major part of this volume deals with the natural climatic phenomena as scientists now understand them. The principal climatic controls will be dealt with first in Chapter 2. The most prominent feature of the circulation of air over the Pacific Ocean in the region of the Hawaiian Islands is the outflow of air from the great region of high pressure that is usually located northeast of Hawai'i. These northeast trades, as they are called, are the prevailing winds in the Islands, present from 85 to 95% of the time in summer, and from 50 to 80% of the time in the winter. They provide the natural air-conditioning of the Islands. However, major storms associated with cold fronts can and do occur, usually in the period from October to March, and there are also smaller circulation patterns caused by land and sea breezes. Hurricanes and tropical storms also affect Hawai'i. These phenomena of pressure systems, of winds and tropical storms, and of the effect of topography on the air flow of the Islands will be discussed in Chapter 2.

The radiation and energy balances of the Islands will be explained in Chapter 3. The sun is earth's primary source of energy, and the importance of the role of solar radiation in climate cannot be overestimated. As the Hawaiian Islands are situated in the tropics, where the sun is high in the sky all year, they receive a wealth of energy from the sun. At the outer edge of the earth's atmosphere, the solar radiation intensity averages about 1.96 cal/cm²/min (calories per square centimeter per minute). Much of the solar radiation is depleted in passing through the earth's atmosphere, but in an average year, Honolulu receives approximately 180,000 calories per square centimeter, similar to the amount received in northern Africa or the Caribbean islands.

The measurement of radiation had to await development of very sensitive instruments, which occurred only in this century. Early in the 1900s, the sugar planters of Hawai'i recognized the importance of solar radiation on the growth of sugarcane, and began to take measurements. For this reason, Hawai'i has a great many solar radiation stations, one of which has a record of more than fifty years.

There are other types of radiation also—terrestrial, or long-wave, and net radiation. These are important in determining the temperature of the air and the amount of energy available at the earth's surface for evaporation and transpiration. Although neither terrestrial nor net radiation is measured routinely in Hawai'i, there are methods of estimating their magnitude. These will be explored in Chapter 3, accompanied by distribution maps.

Air temperature in Hawai'i is also discussed in Chapter 3. The temperature of the air at a place is partly a result of the radiation balance and partly a result of heat energy that is brought from some other place by the wind (advection). Air temperature is also affected by elevation, since temperature decreases with height. Maps of the distribution of mean annual temperatures for the major islands are also shown in Chapter 3.

Chapter 4 concerns water, which is essential to life and is especially vital on small islands like the Hawaiian Islands, where it cannot be imported from neighboring areas. Thus in Hawai'i there has always been great interest in water, and especially that source of all fresh water—rainfall. This was so for the ancient Polynesians and is still true today. We have called Chapter 4 The Water Balance, following the chapter on radiation balance, but of course in nature the two are intimately related, since evaporation of water depends primarily on energy provided by radiation. This chapter deals with the rain that falls from the heavens, the water that evaporates and transpires from vegetated surfaces, and the water than runs off the surface of the earth in streams or percolates through the soil to the groundwater table. We will discuss methods of estimating the water balances of the various islands in this chapter.

Climatologists have always been interested in classifying climates in order to express in simple terms the totality of all of the climatic elements. The first classification of climate was that of the ancient Greeks, as enunciated by Aristotle, and it has survived in popular literature until the present day. The classification was based on distance from the equator, since the Greek word *klima* was defined as the slope of the earth toward the equator. The regions between the tropics of Cancer and Capricorn were called the "torrid zone," the mid-latitudes the "temperate zone," and the polar regions the "frigid zone." Plants, animals, and even people were thought to owe their characteristics to position in these zones. In this classification, Hawai'i belongs in the torrid zone, but the Hawaiian population would probably not agree with this definition, just as the inhabitants of Minnesota would probably not consider their climate "temperate." Twentieth-century climatologists have also tried to classify climates, with varying degrees of success. The classification suggested by the German climatologist Koeppen in the early 1900s, based primarily on temperature, is still the one most commonly used today, although the 1948 classification by the American climatologist Thornthwaite more rationally relates the temperature and precipitation characteristics of a place. In Chapter 4, we discuss briefly these two classifications and how they define the climate of the Big Island.

Chapter 5 looks at climate and human activity. We describe the links between climate and the modern economy in Hawai'i—for example, tourism and agriculture. We look at climate and human comfort and at attempts to harness energy from the wind and the sun, and we also discuss man's negative impacts on climate—for example, pollution of the air and the groundwater.

Has the climate of Hawai'i changed in the past? Is it changing now? Will it change in the future? These are questions we also try to answer. In Chapter 6, the climates of the distant past are discussed, as well as those changes that have occurred during the last hundred years or so, the period of actual measurement of temperature and precipitation.

In Chapter 7, the importance of the Hawaiian climate in scientific research is discussed, especially the role of the two mammoth mountains, Mauna Kea and Mauna Loa. It was at the Mauna Loa Observatory (MLO), above 60% of the earth's atmosphere, that the first regular measurements of atmospheric CO_2 (carbon dioxide) were begun in 1957. The MLO data have been used by scientists throughout the world. The effect of the increasing concentration of CO_2 on world climate is currently being debated by world scientists, and is discussed in Chapter 7. In an appendix, we provide information on where Hawaiian weather and climate data may be obtained.

Early Hawaiian Concepts of Weather and Climate

Most of the material in this book will deal with the Hawaiian climate as it has been revealed by scientific observations—the amount and distribution of rainfall, solar radiation, humidity, wind, and evaporation. Since these natural phenomena of climate existed before measurements were made, it would be interesting to know how the early Polynesian settlers perceived weather and climate. The early inhabitants of Hawai'i lived close to the land and the sea, and were naturally quite aware of climate. Many words in the Hawaiian language refer to climatic elements. The early Hawaiians recognized only two seasons—*kau* when the sun was most directly overhead, the weather warmer, and the trade winds most reliable, and *ho'oilo* when the sun was more southerly, the weather cooler, and the trade winds not so reliable. *Kau* was associated with the months we call May through October and *ho'oilo* from November through April. Modern analysts would agree with the concept of only two seasons but would define them slightly differently—the *kau* season as May–September and the *ho'oilo* as October through April.

Today, climatology as a science depends heavily on a long period of record in order to predict probabilities or frequencies of weather events. The ancient Polynesians, of course, did not have weather records. By observing the various atmospheric changes and the resulting weather events, they mentally cataloged these observations so that a body of orally transmitted weather knowledge was handed down from generation to generation.

The Hawaiians who devoted most of their time to studying climatological changes were called *kilo lani*, seers who had the ability to "tie things together" and predict the future. A *kilo lani* was able to look at the atmosphere, the sky, and the sea and relate what he saw to conditions on land, and thus he could predict what would likely happen in the near future.

The students who were trained by the *kilo lani* were called *'ailolo*. *'Ai* means "to consume"—not only food, but also knowledge. *'Ailolo* means particularly "to commit to memory." (The Pukui-Elbert *Hawaiian Dictionary* further describes it as "skilled, trained, proficient.") *Lolo* means brain. This recall talent of the *'ailolo* could span several years. If a rainstorm had occurred previously accompanied by certain preliminary atmospheric indicators, and these indicators occurred again, the proficient *'ailolo* would be able to predict not only the coming rainstorm but also its characteristics. During each similar occurrence, the *'ailolo* would add to his store of knowledge of this particular event. Through time, the *'ailolo* became quite skilled and were relied upon for their knowledge of things associated with weather events.

It is thought that the ordinary Hawaiian *(maka'āinana)* could "read" the weather and predict what could happen in the next three or four days, but it is believed that the *'ailolo* could do much better. Of course, the *kilo lani, 'ailolo,* and *maka'āinana* were regional experts only. Their folklore and memory encompassed a specific area. A person wanting to know weather conditions or ocean currents off the southern coast of Maui would not consult an *'ailolo* of Honolulu.

It must be mentioned that the *kilo lani* and *'ailolo* were also experts in fields other than climatology. *Kilo lani* literally means a soothsayer who predicts the future by observing the sky, and the "future" could be in many realms. The word *'ailolo* refers to one who is skilled and proficient, whether it be in net making, canoe building, or weather predicting.

Perhaps a few examples will help. As do meteorologists today, the Hawaiians had names for different cloud formations. For example, fair weather cumulus clouds often appear as a set of cumulus clouds of varied size, the so-called cotton-puff clouds. These clouds the Hawaiians referred to as *aopua'a*, where *ao* means cloud and *pua'a* means pig. The mental association of the early Hawaiians was a mother pig-cloud with small piglet-clouds following her. It isn't difficult to see the analogy! The Kona Coast is famous for these *aopua'a* cloud formations. This kind of cloud portended good weather, with no sign of any impending storms.

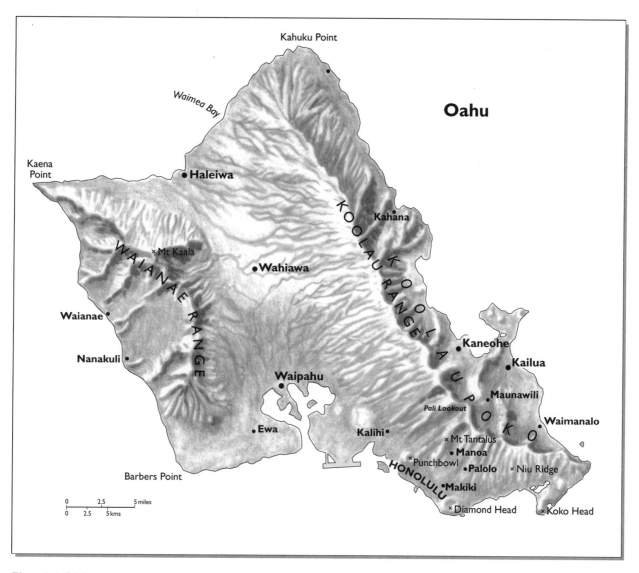

Figure 1.4 O'ahu

Another cloud formation was called *aopehupehu*. *Pehu* means "to swell up." *Aopehupehu* means a cloud which is causing itself to expand and swell up. In other words, these are developing cumulus clouds which are continually growing. In Hawai'i, especially during the summer, the skies are often filled with *aopehupehu*. As these clouds drift with the northeast trade winds toward O'ahu, they take up more moisture. This moisture creates a tinge of darkness which appears at the base of the cloud. As the cloud blows over the crest of the Ko'olau mountains, rain starts to fall from it. Much of the rain falls on the leeward side of the crest and keeps the leeward mountain valleys such as Mānoa, Kalihi, and Pālolo lush and green. If there are heavier, darker clouds in great numbers, the Hawaiians observed that most of the rainfall occurred at lower elevations and stayed on the windward side of the island.

In addition, clouds were named after their color by the early Hawaiians. A black cloud was termed *'ele'ele;* a white cloud, *ke'oke'o.* Also, clouds were named according to their character: a sheltering cloud, *ho'omalumalu* and a threatening cloud, *ho'oweliweli.*

The early inhabitants paid special attention to the aspect of the sky. If the sky in the western horizon was blue-black *(uliuli)* at sunset, it was said to be *pāuli* and was regarded as prognosticating a high surf, *kaiko'o.* If there was an opening in the cloud, like the jaw of the swordfish, it was called *'ena* and was considered a sign of rain. If the sky was entirely overcast with almost no wind, it was said to be *po'ipū* (shut up, covered over entirely). If the wind started up, the expression *ho'okaka'a* (a rolling together) was used. If the clouds that covered the sky were exceedingly black, it was thought that *Kūlanihāko'i* (a mythical pond or lake in the sky), was in them. *Kūlanihāko'i* was the place where thunder, lightning, wind, rain, and violent storms originated.

The general Hawaiian term for rain is *ua.* The Hawaiian climatologist was very precise and called *ua* by many different names, usually taking into consideration location, temperature, density, and so forth. An example of this is the word *'awa,* which describes cold mountain rain, fog, or mist. A continuous rain was called *ua ho'okina,* a downpour *ua lanipili.* *Kualau* describes the rain which occurs at sea and which is usually associated with wind. The ancient Hawaiians designated appropriately the varieties of rain peculiar to each part of the island coast or valleys. The rain in Mānoa was called *ua Kuahine* and in Hana, Maui, *ua lani ha'aha'a.* A rainbow,

anuenue, was an especially favorable omen to the early Hawaiians, symbolizing the presence of the gods.

They noted that if rain was accompanied by wind, thunder, lightning, and perhaps a rainbow, the storm would probably not continue long, but if the rain was unaccompanied by wind, it would probably be prolonged. When the western horizon was red at sunset, its appearance was termed *aka'ula* (red shadow or glow), and this was looked upon as a sign that the rain would stop. A protracted rainstorm was called *ualoa,* one of short duration was known as *uapoko,* and a cold rain was termed *uahea.*

The Hawaiians called wind in general *makani,* a variable wind *makani pōlua,* and a fair wind *makani 'olu'olu.* They used several words for the northeast trade wind: *Moa'e, A'e, A'e Loa, Mao'e Lehua,* and *Mao'e pehu.* Winds from the leeward direction were called Kona winds. A number of wind names were associated with specific places: *'Alahonua* with Hilo, *Āpa'apa'a* with Kohala on the Big Island, *Alahou* with Moloka'i, *Kaua'ula* with Lahaina in Maui, and *'Āhiu* with Kahana in O'ahu.

The Hawaiian word for sea is *kai* or *moana.* For the Polynesians, *kai* is the visible sea, the sea you can work, play, fish, and sail in. The sea beyond the horizon is the *moana,* the endless sea. This is similar to the English usage of the words ocean and sea, where ocean is *moana* and sea is *kai.*

Most Polynesians consider the *kai* as part of the family. For example, a brother is *kaikane,* sister, *kaikuahine,* cousin, *kaikunāne* (male cousin of a female), and so forth. The sea became a relative in the Hawaiian's mind because it was the source of their original sustenance, original in the sense that when the Hawaiians first came to the Islands there were no planted crops and no animals for husbandry. They had to depend mainly upon the waters and reefs close to the Islands for their protein. On the other hand, the climatological significance of the *moana* is its warm temperature, derived from the Pacific Equatorial Drift, which bathes the Islands and helps keep the temperature balmy and comfortable.

Many place names in the Hawaiian language have weather-related meanings. For example, *Mauna Kea,* which means "white mountain," refers to the snowcapped summit of that volcano, and *Pukalani,* a town on the northwest slope of Haleakalā in Maui, means "hole in the sky." Rainy *Wai'ale'ale,* on Kauai, has the literal Hawaiian meaning of "overflowing water."

CHAPTER 2

Climate Controls

Thomas Schroeder

Large Scale Controls

In Hawai'i the principal climatic controls are the position of the Islands on the earth's surface, the trade winds, the winter storms, the infrequent tropical disturbances, and the topography of the Islands. In this chapter we discuss these and other elements that contribute to Hawaiian climate.

The sun is the energy source for the earth's atmosphere. Radiation balance studies comparing incoming solar radiation to what is lost by infrared radiation indicate that the surface of the earth is constantly warming by radiation, while the atmosphere is constantly cooling. (The radiation and energy balances of the Hawaiian Islands are dealt with in Chapter 3.) Since the temperatures of both the surface and the atmosphere vary little, other mechanisms must be at work to maintain the thermal balance. Surface energy is transferred to the atmosphere by the mechanisms of conduction (direct transfer by contact) or convection (mass motions of the air). In the open atmosphere conduction is inefficient, so the atmosphere transfers energy by vertical motions. An analogy is the transfer of heat from a burner through a pan of water in the process of boiling.

Comparing radiation balances for various latitudinal bands, we find that the regions between 35° north and south latitudes have radiation surpluses, while polar regions have deficits. The mechanisms that transfer this energy are the horizontal motions in the atmosphere—the winds and the ocean currents. A northern hemisphere anticyclone, or high-pressure area, has northerly winds on its eastern flank and southerly winds on its western flank. North winds carry cold air equatorward, while south winds carry warm air poleward. The result is a reduction of temperature contrasts between equator and pole. Large ocean circulations operate in the same manner.

The average atmospheric motion over a period of months to years is referred to as the general circulation. General circulation maps are statistical products, and they never exactly match the daily weather map as shown on television or in the daily newspaper. We shall discuss the principal features of the general circulation influencing Hawaiian climate and the nature of deviations from the mean.

General Circulation

The earth's general circulation consists of three meridional (aligned along a meridian) cells, as seen in Figure 2.1. Warm air rises near the equator and moves poleward at high altitudes. This air sinks near 30°N latitude and returns to the equator at the surface. This system is called the Hadley Cell, in honor of the seventeenth century English scientist who first proposed it. Hawai'i lies within the influence of the Hadley Cell. As the air moves equatorward from the center of the sinking motion, the subtropical high-pressure center, it is deflected by the earth's rotation and becomes a northeasterly wind. During the Age of Discovery sailing vessels made

use of these winds, which the sailors named the trade winds.

The trade winds dominate the tropical oceans outside of the monsoon regions of Asia and Africa. They are so constant that some geographical features are named according to the properties of the trades (e.g., the Windward and Leeward Antilles of the Caribbean and windward and leeward O'ahu in Hawai'i). Weather in the trade wind regions is fairly uniform, though subtle day-to-day variations do occur.

A feature of the trade wind regions is the trade wind inversion. Sinking air in the Hadley Cell warms due to compression. At the point of contact with warm air rising from the surface and cooling, a layer forms in which warm air overlies cool air. Such a layer is termed a temperature inversion. A number of mechanisms create temperature inversions, but no lower atmospheric inversion is as persistent or dominates the climate as much as the trade wind inversion (Figure 2.2). Buoyant air carried aloft starts to lose buoyancy at the inversion, where it finds itself cooler and denser than the surrounding air. Air above the inversion is quite dry and any

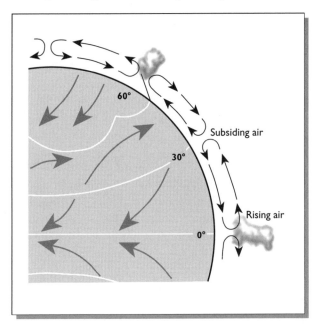

Figure 2.1 Idealized Hadley Cell, showing vertical and horizontal wind patterns

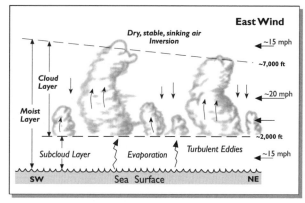

Figure 2.2 Generalized trade wind weather as air moves from northeast to southwest (after Malkus, 1958)

cloud penetrating the inversion rapidly evaporates. The trade wind inversion is revealed by the nearly flat cloud tops that can be seen from jet aircraft flying in the Hawaiian latitudes, as well as in the sharp changes in local climate along the slopes of the high volcanoes extending above the inversion. The mean inversion height over Hawai'i is approximately 2 km (6,560 ft), although it varies considerably from day to day.

The inversion marks the lower boundary of air subsiding in the North Pacific subtropical anticyclone. Surface air in the anticyclone first flows toward the western continental coast, where it is cooled and stabilized by the upwelling water.

The inversion may sink to the surface, with clouds absent or scattered. Then, as the direction becomes more easterly and the air leaves the coast and moves toward Hawai'i, it passes over warmer water and the surface layer grows in thickness. Extensive shallow-layer clouds (stratocumulus) develop. Still farther west, where the surface heating rate diminishes, clouds align themselves in organized patterns. Rain falls from very few of these clouds. In general the trade wind belt is dry. The trade winds lie in latitudes similar to the great subtropical Sahara and Sonoran deserts. Rainfall over the Hawaiian Islands is much greater than over the surrounding oceans as a result of the interaction of the trade winds with the mountainous islands, as we shall explain.

The trade winds vary over the course of a year. They are most common in summer and least common in winter. For example, winds from the east and northeast (the directions from which the trade winds blow) occur 92% of the time in August, but only 50% of the time in January in Honolulu. Trade wind weather is characterized by steady winds, pleasant temperatures and humidities, and a strong diurnal variation of clouds and rainfall. When the trades fail, the weather can become unpleasant, characterized by variable winds, high humidities,

and heavy rains. Occasionally large storm systems may visit the Islands, producing damaging winds, heavy rains, and other severe weather. Later in this chapter we shall discuss these events.

Another large-scale control is the prevailing anticyclonic circulation within the northern Pacific Ocean. The Hawaiian Islands lie in the path of the oceanic North Equatorial Current, which is an oceanic analog to the trade winds. This current transports relatively cool water from the northeastern Pacific and helps maintain the equable temperatures in Hawai'i year round, since the annual range of ocean temperature is only 3 °C (5 °F). Furthermore, air approaching the Islands from any direction must traverse 3,800 km (2,400 mi) of ocean (Figure 1.1). Arctic air approaching in winter is warmed as much as 25 °C (45 °F) and tropical air is cooled.

The Annual Cycle and Interannual Variability

The annual cycle of the northeast Pacific is best demonstrated by comparing the extremes. Figure 2.3 depicts the mean sea level pressure patterns and winds for January and July. In January, the subtropical high-pressure area lies near 32 °N, 130 °W; the central pressure is 1,021 mb. In July, the center is near 38 °N, 150 °W and the central pressure is 1,025 mb. In January the axis of high pressure, or ridge, extends westward from the center to just north of the Islands. Since the January map represents average conditions, the ridge actually moves north and south of the mean position. When the ridge is near the Islands, winds are lighter than normal. The subsidence is stronger, hence the inversion is stronger. When the ridge moves south of Hawai'i, the winds may be variable. In contrast, the July pressure ridge lies well north of the Islands, the trade winds are steady, and local weather is constant.

The January maps represent an average of several

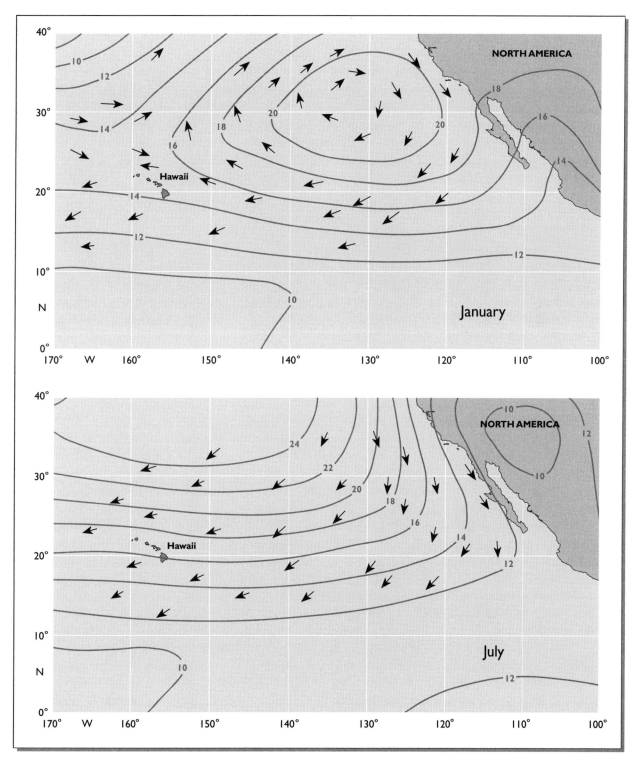

Figure 2.3 Average January and July sea level pressure and surface winds in the northeast Pacific Ocean. (Units of pressure are millibars (mb) above 1000 mb. For example, 20 = 1020 mb.)

weather systems that influence Hawai'i in the cool season. These include stationary highs, migratory highs, migratory cyclonic storms (or low-pressure systems), and frontal systems. These systems are most active in January and are absent in July. Hawai'i lies at the southern end of the North Pacific winter storm track.

Although weather in Hawai'i is usually described as uniform, there are significant year-to-year variations. This can be seen in the January rainfalls for the past twenty years at the University of Hawaii's Department of Meteorology, which lies 4 km (2.4 mi) inland from Waikīkī Beach (Figure 2.4). In twenty years of record, January rainfall exceeded 200 mm (8 in) seven times, yet in eight years it was less than 50 mm (2 in). The mean value was seldom approached, with fifteen years far above or below the average.

The data in Figure 2.4 illustrate the interannual variability of Hawaiian weather. What accounts for this variability? During the cool season the subtropical ridge lies near the Islands. Interannual variability of the ridge position accompanies wide swings in the cool wet-season weather pattern, since a ridge

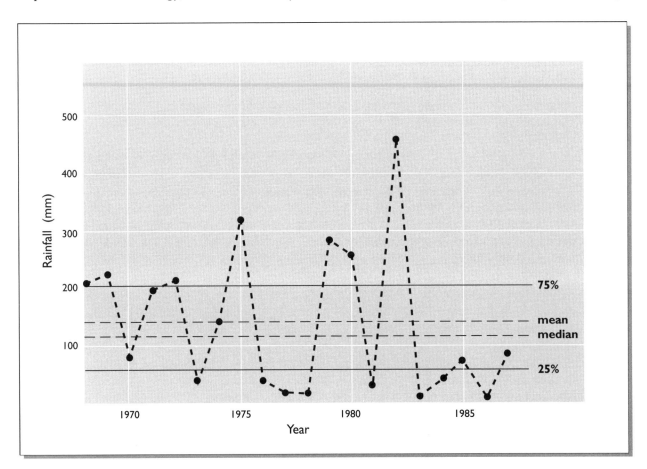

Figure 2.4 January rainfall (mm) for the University of Hawaii, Department of Meteorology weather station, 1968–1987

south of Hawai'i allows more fronts and storms. If the ridge lies north of the Islands, trade wind weather persists; if the ridge lies directly over the Islands, winds are light and clouds absent.

Interannual variability of Hawaiian cool-season rainfall is only one manifestation of large-scale atmospheric circulation changes affecting the entire Pacific Basin. The South Pacific atmosphere experiences a basin-wide oscillation in sea level pressure named the Southern Oscillation. At opposite ends of a large seesaw are the high-pressure center near Easter Island in the southeast Pacific and a low-pressure center over Indonesia, the "maritime continent" on the western boundary of the region. Sea level pressure changes at the two centers are negatively correlated; i.e., a rise in pressure at the low center accompanies a fall of pressure in the high. During these periods of negative phases of the Southern Oscillation, major changes in the equatorial winds and sea surface temperatures occur. Warming in the equatorial central Pacific shifts the rising motion in the Hadley Cell nearer the equator. The sinking center or subtropical ridge shifts closer to the Islands, and dry conditions prevail (Figure 2.5). The warming of the sea surface has been termed "El Niño" after an annual sea surface warming along the west coast of equatorial South America. Nearly all major statewide Hawaiian droughts have coincided with El Niño events, as seen in Table 1. The El Niño events of 1877–1878, 1982–1983, 1986–1987, and 1991–1992 all coincided with significant dry spells in Hawai'i.

Researchers are currently exploring details of the El Niño–Southern Oscillation (ENSO) phenomenon as well as other features of interannual climate variability. We may gain insight that could lead to the development of meaningful climate prediction, from which mankind would benefit significantly.

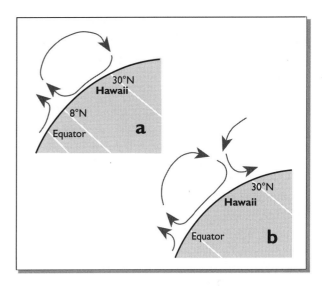

Figure 2.5 Latitudinal location of Hadley cells for normal (a) and El Niño (b) years

Table 1 The Ten Driest Years in Hawai'i: 1890–1980

Percentile Rank	Year	El Niño Event
1	1897	1896–1897
2	1926	1925–1926
3	1919	1918–1919
4	1953	1953
5	1912	1911–1912
6	1941	1941
7	1903	1902–1903
8	1905	1905
9	1977	1976–1977
10	1925	1925–1926

Source: C. S. Ramage, personal communication

Synoptic Climatology

Synoptic meteorology is the study of weather systems which have spatial dimensions of 1,000 to 4,000 km (600–2,400 mi) and last for a few days to one week. These are the features depicted on the routine weather map or "synoptic" analysis, and include migratory highs and lows, frontal systems, tropical cyclones, and upper-tropospheric disturbances. Each is a significant element of Hawaiian climate.

While the North Pacific summer time high-pressure center is nearly stationary, persisting for months at a time, winter time high-pressure systems move past the Islands following the winter cold fronts. The central pressure of these highs can exceed the means of either Figure 2.3 or 2.4. If the centers pass north of the Islands, the winds are still referred to as trades even though they differ from the classical trades described earlier, and indeed, they may exceed gale force. In December 1978, "trades" associated with a strong winter high gusted to 135 km/hr (84 mph) at Waikoloa Village on the island of Hawai'i. These winter "trades" carry evaporatively cooled air from mountain showers over Honolulu, producing a windchill easily noticed by the residents.

A cold front may cross the Islands ahead of a migratory high. These fronts extend from large extratropical lows that lie well northeast of Hawai'i. If the low is near the Islands (Figure 2.6, upper), the winds may blow strongly from the southwest and the Islands may experience heavy showers and severe weather. As the front passes, the winds veer first to the northwest, then north, and finally to northeast as the high moves by the Islands. Leeward sections of the Islands, now exposed to the winds, receive most of their rain from these fronts. Although the rest of an island such as O'ahu may have a near-normal rainfall year, deficient frontal activity may cause a drought in the leeward regions of the island. The distance between drought and normal rainfall regions may be only 10 to 20 km (6 to 12 mi). If the low is far to the northeast (Figure 2.6, lower), the front will bring easterly winds, becoming northeasterly as the front passes. Although these winds are less spectacular, the fronts produce clouds and rain

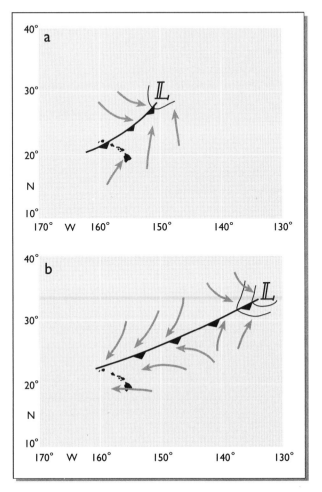

Figure 2.6 Two cold frontal patterns for the Hawaiian Islands. (a) Nearby low with southwesterly winds. (b) "Shear line" configuration with distant low and easterly winds

efficiently. While perhaps these are not classic trade winds, the weather pattern so produced is sometimes referred to as "wet trades." In an average winter, fifteen frontal systems may pass Līhu'e, Kaua'i. Of these, thirteen may reach Honolulu, ten Kahului, Maui, and nine Hilo on the Big Island.

Due to the modifying effects of the surrounding ocean, the changes in temperature as a front passes are minor compared to those in mid-latitudes, but local people notice the change. The absence of strong frontal systems is one consequence of El Niño conditions.

Kona Lows and Kona Weather

A Kona storm is a low-pressure system which develops in the upper troposphere, gradually extends to lower altitudes, and may eventually appear as a low at the earth's surface. If such a system develops to the west of Hawai'i, moist, showery southerly winds (Figure 2.7) may persist for more than a week, and rainfall totals are often large. In January 1980, 1,270 mm (50 in) of rain fell on Haleakalā, Maui in three days. Flooding, high winds, and high surf associated with this weather can damage property. A nearby extratropical low may produce similar features. Kona storms form near the Islands every year but locations and effects vary. In the drought winter of 1976–1977, as seen in Table 1, several Kona storms formed east of the Islands, and rain fell on the ocean. A winter with weak frontal activity and no Kona storms may cause a serious drought in leeward portions of Hawai'i.

"Kona weather" is a term used to describe periods of light, variable winds. This typically occurs when the subtropical ridge lies over the state. Solar heating over the land produces sea breezes by day, and nocturnal cooling produces land breezes. Afternoon clouds forming over interior sections and mountain slopes often produce showers. Kona weather dominates the Kona Coast of the island of Hawai'i, since the massive dome of Mauna Loa shelters that region from the prevailing trades.

Tropical Cyclones

Tropical cyclones form over the warm oceans above five degrees of latitude from the equator. They are more compact and more intense than extratropical cyclones, or Kona lows. If winds exceed 64 km/hr (38 mph), the system is called a tropical storm and is given a name. If winds exceed 105 km/hr (63 mph), the storm attains hurricane status. West of 180° longitude (the international date line) the storm is called a typhoon, while storms near Hawai'i are called hurricanes.

The primary spawning grounds for northeast Pacific hurricanes are the tropical waters west of Central America. On average, between May and December, sixteen tropical storms form north of the equator and east of 140°W (the eastern Pacific hurricane region); of these, eight become hurricanes. As they move north and west of their birthplace, most storms encounter unfavorable atmospheric and/or oceanic conditions, and then decay. A few, however, reach the area west of 140°W and enter the central Pacific hurricane region. The National Weather Service Forecast Office in Honolulu then becomes the Central Pacific Hurricane Center. Occasionally a storm forms in the central Pacific. These rare events earn Hawaiian names. Annually, approximately three tropical storms either enter or form in the central Pacific (Figure 2.8), but severe storms are rare. Since 1957 only four hurricanes have had major impact on the Islands.

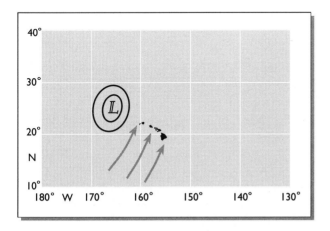

Figure 2.7 A Kona low west of the Islands causing a moist southerly flow over the State

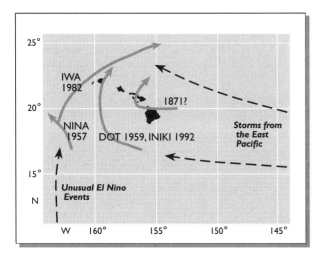

Figure 2.8 Tropical cyclone tracks over the central Pacific Ocean. The dashed arrows indicate "typical" tracks. Solid lines are for specific cases; Nina 1957, Dot 1959, Iwa 1982, and Iniki 1992, and the unnamed Kohala storm of 1871.

These were Nina (1957), Dot (1959), Iwa (1982), and Iniki (1992). Iwa was a weak, decaying storm which brushed Kaua'i on 23 November 1982, but damage approached $250 million. Iniki's winds at landfall were 210 km/hr (130 mph) with gusts of 258 km/hr (160 mph). (These are estimates for winds near the ground over open terrain.) Higher gusts occurred in mountainous sections of Kaua'i. The center of the storm (the eye) crossed over the western end of Kaua'i, exiting the north shore west of Princeville. At the time this book was going to press, damage surveys were not complete but preliminary estimates placed the value between $2 billion and $3 billion. (Insurance claims alone have exceeded $1.6 billion.)

Hurricane damage may arise from winds, rains, tornadoes, coastal storm surges, and high surf. In the instances of Iwa and Iniki primary damage sources were wind and the additive effects of coastal surge and wave action. Hawaiian houses have been built for maximum ventilation and use lightweight

materials. Roofs have proven especially vulnerable. Property on the south shore of Kaua'i was severely damaged during both Iwa and Iniki. During Iniki the surge was about 1.5 m (4.9 ft), but superimposed waves and resulting overwash drove water to extreme heights of 8.7 m (28.5 ft). Water penetrated 300 m (1,000 ft) inland. The State of Hawaii is now reevaluating building codes and coastal zone management policies in light of Iniki. Iniki is the greatest natural disaster in the history of the state. Fortunately, adequate warning by the Central Pacific Hurricane Center and preparedness by civil defense agencies saved many lives.

Upper-tropospheric Disturbances

In the atmosphere over Hawai'i, surface trade winds may underlie markedly different upper-tropospheric systems. Troughs in the upper troposphere at an altitude of about 11 km (35,000 ft) may develop near or pass over the Islands throughout the year. At times the trough may penetrate downward as a Kona low, but more often the trough has a less-obvious effect on the surface weather. The upward motion associated with the trough (Figure 2.9) may suffice to lift or even eliminate the trade wind inversion. Then the lower troposphere over Hawai'i nearly always contains enough moisture for heavy rain to fall.

On April 19, 1974, an upper-tropospheric trough passed over low-level easterly winds, and thunderstorms formed over the mountains of Kaua'i and O'ahu. More than 500 mm (20 in) of rain fell on O'ahu in 24 hours (Figure 2.10), 114 mm (4.5 in) falling in one hour. Five people died in the resulting floods. Again, between January 10 and 17, 1979, an upper-tropospheric trough enhanced rain from strong post-frontal northeasterly winds, and 1,778 mm (70 in) of rain fell at 'O'ōkala on the northeast coast of the island of Hawai'i.

Upper-tropospheric troughs are year-round fea-

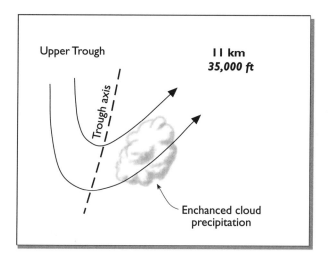

Figure 2.9 The wind pattern at a height of 11 kilometers (35,000 feet) in an upper-tropospheric trough

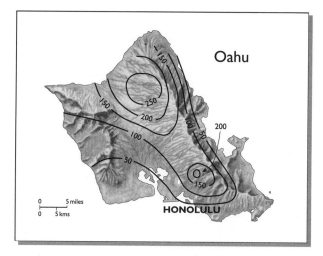

Figure 2.10 Thirteen-hour rainfall (mm) on Oʻahu during the storm of 19 April 1974 (after Schroeder, 1977a)

tures of the Hawaiian climate. In summer they are a primary source of trade wind rainfall. In extreme instances they support the development of thunderstorms with trade winds, a phenomenon not mentioned in most textbooks on tropical meteorology.

Ocean Waves—Hawaiian Surf

The Hawaiian Islands lie in the largest ocean on the planet. Open-ocean swells breaking over fringing reefs create the world-famous Hawaiian surf. Exceptionally large waves modify the shoreline and may damage shoreline properties. During high surf, the surf zone is extremely dangerous, and an important function of the National Weather Service Forecast Office at Honolulu is issuing high surf advisories.

Winds blowing over the ocean surface generate waves. Wave size depends on the strength of the wind and expanse of ocean over which the winds blow in a straight line (the fetch). As waves leave the generation region, they gradually lose energy. A forecaster must determine the size of the waves that will reach the Islands and the time of arrival. As the waves encounter gradually rising ocean bottoms, they grow in size and eventually break as surf (Figure 2.11). The size of the waves along a given stretch of coast depends on the direction of the arriving waves and the local coastal topography. At Waimea Bay, on the north shore of Oʻahu, surf is generally small, but some of the largest surf in the world may accompany a north swell at this location.

Hawaiian surf has an annual cycle. During the northern hemisphere winter, North Pacific extratropical cyclones generate swells that arrive at the

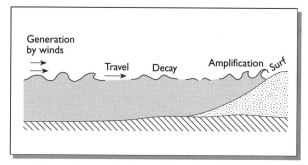

Figure 2.11 The life of ocean waves as they form, decay, and amplify as surf

Islands with heights of 2 to 4 m (6 to 8 ft). Upon reaching the north and west shores of the Islands, they become surf 4 to 6 m (12 to 18 ft) in height. Trade winds generate smaller swells throughout the year. During the southern hemisphere winter, storms far beyond the equator generate swells which reach Hawai'i from the south. These waves are smaller than the north swells because they travel farther and have more time to decay. The resulting surf is easier for surfers to ride and therefore quite popular. Damaging surf arises from extremely strong extratropical cyclones that pass nearby, from Kona storms, and from the rare hurricane.

Mesoscale Influences

Mesoscale meteorology is the study of atmospheric circulation systems with spatial scales of a few km to a few hundred km, and temporal scales of hours to a few days. In Hawai'i the combination of mountainous islands and persistent trade winds creates mesoscale systems that dominate local climate.

If the mountains are below the inversion, a substantial amount of trade wind air will pass over the barrier. This is the case for O'ahu, where the maximum elevation in the windward Ko'olau Range is 960 m (3,150 ft) (Figure 2.12). On the island of Hawai'i, Mauna Loa and Mauna Kea are more formidable barriers. Most trade wind air is diverted

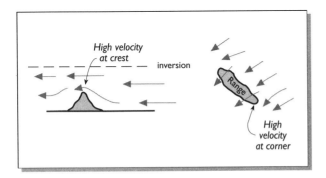

Figure 2.12 Air flow over and around a low island such as O'ahu

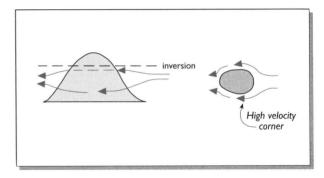

Figure 2.13 Air flow over and around an island mountain such as Mauna Loa

around these mountains except for a small amount that penetrates the high, 2 km (6600 ft) saddle between them (Figure 2.13).

In both cases the air passing over the barriers is orographically lifted. As the air rises it cools, and clouds form along the slope (Figure 2.14). These clouds bring the moisture that creates the rain forest climates along the mountain slopes. Vegetation also intercepts cloud vapor, which precipitates as fog drip. On the Big Island, where the mountains extend above the inversion, deserts occupy their summits. Extraction of moisture from the air stream as it is lifted along the windward slopes leads to the creation of dry zones in the leeward "rain shadow." The topography of the Islands, the nature of the orographic effect, and the inversion create numerous microclimates. One may drive 25 km (15 mi) from Honoka'a to Waimea on the Big Island, and pass from lush sugar fields to rain forests in orographic fog to prickly pear cactus.

As the air passes over or around the island mountains, it accelerates as a result of the pressure of the air overtaking it from upstream. We find higher wind speeds at mountain crests such as the Ko'olau ridge on O'ahu, in the saddles between mountains (e.g., the Waimea and Humu'ula saddles of the Big Island or the central valley of Maui), in notches in the ridges (the Pali Lookout on O'ahu), and the

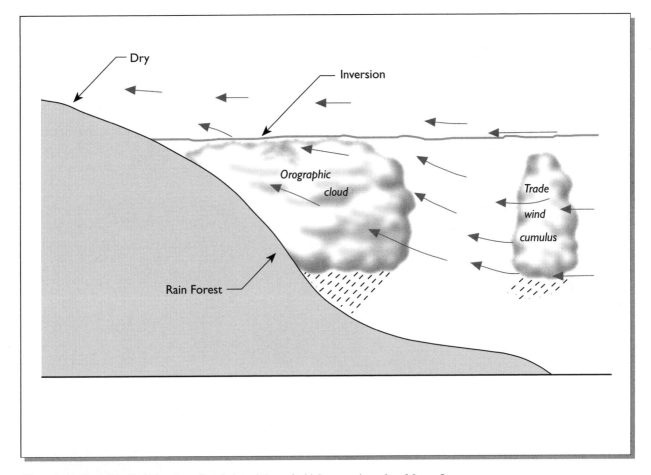

Dry

Inversion

Orographic cloud

Trade wind cumulus

Rain Forest

Figure 2.14 Generalized weather along the windward slope of a high mountain such as Mauna Loa

ocean channels between the Islands. Islanders are using these high wind areas to generate energy, as will be explained in Chapter 5. Agriculture has not prospered in these windy regions, nor do people find them enjoyable living areas. Over the ocean, the windy channels are hazardous for navigation. As air passes the corner of an obstacle, eddies (rotary wind systems) may form. In these eddies the winds may counter the prevailing trade wind flow, producing sharp contrasts in wind climate. The best-known eddy in Hawai'i is the "Maui Vortex," which forms along the northwest flank of Haleakalā (Figure 2.15). The vortex is a daily feature of trade wind weather on Maui and is described in detail in a later chapter.

When two air streams converge, the accumulation of mass must be relieved. The solution is for the air to move vertically. For surface wind convergence, the result is rising motion and, given adequate moisture, cloud formation. In Hawai'i, surface wind convergence occurs in several ways. Windward of the Big Island, air slows as it meets the

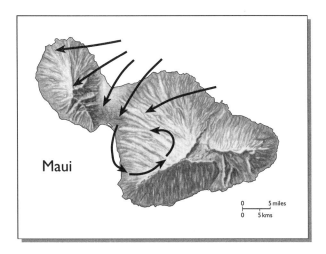

Figure 2.15 The Maui vortex: air spinning in a cyclonic pattern along the northwest slope of Haleakalā

barrier, while air upstream overtakes it. A band of clouds forms resembling the bow wave of a ship moving through water (Figure 2.16). At night, land breezes enhance the convergence with resulting clouds and rainfall.

Air streams converge as they flow around opposing corners of a mountain barrier. On Moloka'i (Figure 2.17), a persistent cloud band forms over West Moloka'i as air passing north and south of the higher mass of east Moloka'i converges. This cloud plume may extend 100 km (60 mi) beyond the island. At the southwest corner of Mauna Loa, the trades passing the corner converge with the leeward sea breeze. This cloud band is evident on satellite photographs and causes a local rainfall maximum. A similar plume, over southwest Haleakalā in Maui, extends to the neighboring island of Kaho'olawe.

Under certain conditions, air moving over a mountain barrier accelerates as it returns to the surface on the leeward side, as happens in winter over the Front Range of the North American Rockies, in the Alps of Europe, and in Hawai'i. The maximum surface wind gust recorded on January 14, 1970, on

O'ahu was 155 km/hr (93 mph) on the northeast coast, when 70 km/hr (42 mph) westerly winds passed over the Ko'olau Range. During Hurricane Iwa the most severe wind damage on O'ahu occurred downwind of each mountain range (Figure 2.18). Damaging downslope winds have also occurred on Maui and Hawai'i.

Thermal Circulations

Soil has a lower heat capacity than water. About five times as much heat must be applied to a volume of water to attain the same temperature increase as that of an equal volume of soil. Soil also conducts heat poorly, and heat absorbed by the soil is retained near the surface. In June 1980, meteorologists from the University of Hawaii measured temperatures in ash at the Mauna Kea summit. On a clear day the diurnal temperature range was 35 °C (63 °F) at a 6 mm (.25 in) depth, and only 9 °C (16 °F) at a 165 mm (6.5 in) depth, as seen in Figure 2.19.

In contrast, water readily conducts and convects heat vertically. As a result, solar heating during the day causes temperatures of the land surface and the adjacent air over land to exceed that of nearby coastal waters. This temperature difference produces a pressure imbalance that drives cool air shoreward as a sea breeze. In the evening, land cools more rapidly than the ocean, causing the air temperatures over land to drop below those over the coastal waters, and cool air is driven seaward as a land breeze (Figure 2.20).

The argument above for thermal differences between land and water applies as well to differences between land and air. Air is a poor conductor of heat and a poor absorber of solar radiation. During the day a mountain slope will warm more than the surrounding air. Air rises along the slope as a valley breeze (Figure 2.21). At night the process reverses and a mountain breeze (drainage wind) moves down the slope. The drainage wind is easy to visualize.

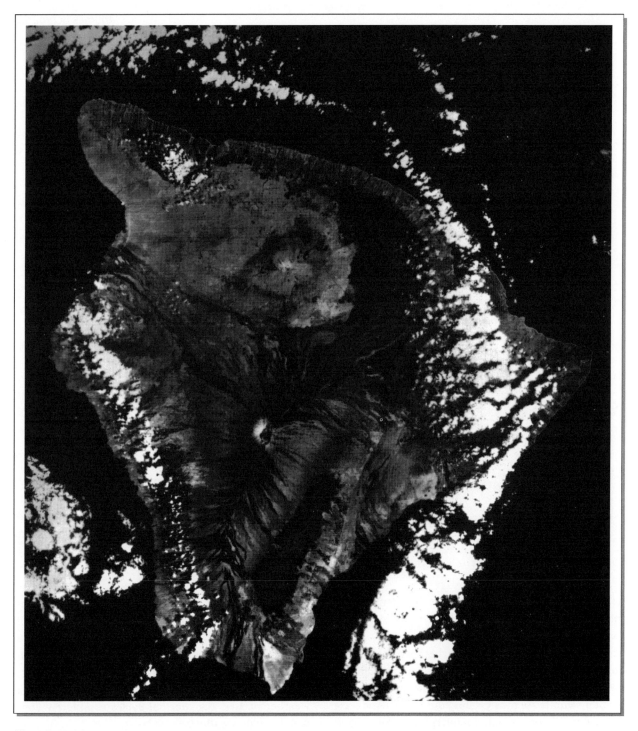

Figure 2.16 Satellite image of the island of Hawai'i showing the "bow wave" cloud along the windward coast

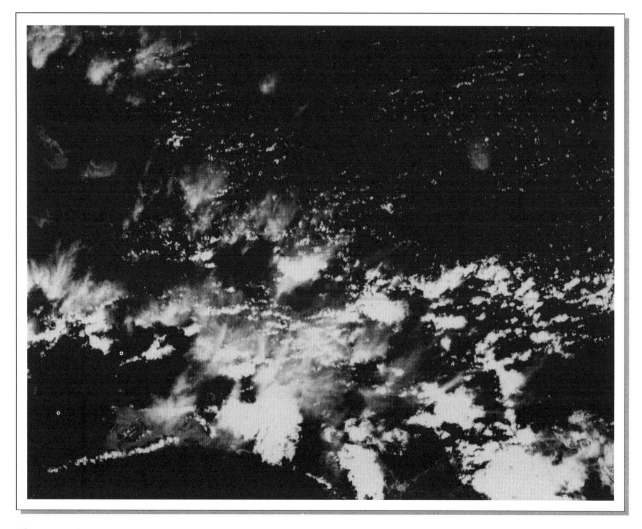

Figure 2.17 Satellite image of Molokaʻi and Maui with the Molokaʻi cloud plume extending over the waters downwind

The air near the slope is cooler and thus denser than the surrounding air, and it moves much as a lava flow moves down the flanks of a volcano.

The Hawaiian Islands have both coastal zones and large mountains, and on any given day the two mechanisms described above may be at work. On smaller islands such as Oʻahu, the trade winds are generally strong enough to overpower these local influences. On the island of Hawaiʻi, which features the most massive mountains on earth, these local winds dominate the daily weather pattern. Some regular sea breezes occur on all major islands, though the extent of the circulation may be limited. When the synoptic-scale winds fail, and Kona weather occurs, the thermal cycles completely control the daily weather.

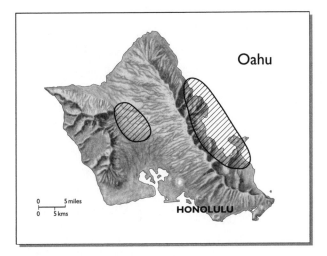

Figure 2.18 O'ahu regions, lee of mountains in westerly winds, which experience significant damage during strong westerly wind patterns

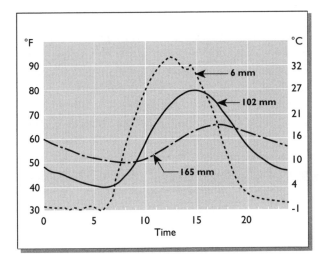

Figure 2.19 Soil temperatures at different depths at the summit of Mauna Kea, June 1980

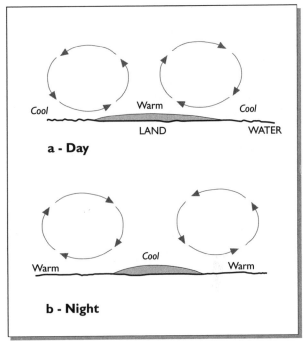

Figure 2.20 Land and sea breeze circulation patterns

The diurnal variation of cloudiness and rainfall within the trade winds belt away from land is characterized by a nocturnal maximum. The most frequently cited cause is radiative cooling of cloud tops, which causes the overturning of cooled cloud-top air and thus enhances cloud development. On the Big Island, several different diurnal variation patterns are evident (Figure 2.22). While diurnal rainfall patterns appear on each island, the strongest temporal and spatial variations occur on the Big Island.

At windward sites such as Hilo, rain most often falls (25% of the time) near midnight. The open ocean maximum occurs near sunrise. At Hilo a drainage wind from Mauna Loa and Mauna Kea develops every evening, and is the most frequently observed wind there. The drainage enhances shower activity at the offshore convergence band. Farther up slope, the primary rain producer is the orographic cloud mass that develops during daylight as land/mountain breezes yield to sea/valley breezes. Near the 2 km (6,600 ft) elevation, a late afternoon rainfall maximum occurs. At leeward sites, clouds

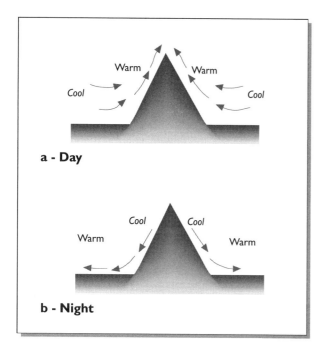

Figure 2.21 Valley and mountain breeze circulation patterns along a slope

develop as a result of the afternoon sea breeze interacting with trade winds crossing the saddles. Here, an afternoon rainfall maximum is pronounced. In nine years of July records at Kealakekua (Kona), no measurable rain fell between 9:00 and 10:00 A.M. In the annual mean, the ratio of maximum to minimum hourly rainfall frequency at that site is 13:1. These regular diurnal weather cycles are some of the most fascinating aspects of weather in the trade wind regions.

Severe Local Storms

Although the Hawaiian climate is generally pleasant, violent weather may occur. About five times a year torrential rains cause sufficient damage to merit mention in the climatological records. Lives have been lost. The torrential rain threat is greatest near the mountains, since persistent winds which continually form precipitating clouds can become anchored to a topographical feature. The lava rocks which comprise the mountains can absorb several centimeters of rain over several hours, but once the rock becomes saturated, the resulting flash floods can reach coastal areas in one hour. Some extreme rainfall totals include 965 mm (38 in) in 24 hours at Kīlauea Plantation, Kaua'i; 406 mm (16 in) in 6 hours at Maunawili, O'ahu; and 114 mm (4.5 in) in one hour and 51 mm (2 in) in less than 10 minutes, at Helemano Intake, O'ahu. The flood hazard is especially great in remote valleys where communications are limited. The extreme weather gradients create situations in which the distance from fine weather to flood may be only a few kilometers. Hikers venturing into isolated mountainous areas are particularly vulnerable to this hazard.

A hazard known as a "straight line" wind arises from major storms with strong trade winds. As discussed previously, leeward areas and island "corners" are highly vulnerable to such winds. Strong winds like these produce structural damage ranging from loss of a few shingles to loss of roofs and entire structures. Trees falling on power lines cause power outages. A squall line of storms associated with Hurricane Iwa downed the major electric power transmission lines connecting the main generating plant on O'ahu to the island's electrical grid. The island suffered power outages for several days, and since O'ahu is isolated from any neighboring power generation facilities, power was restored only when equipment was repaired. Potential wind damage, however, is seldom a design criterion for Hawaiian houses. Structural failure due to wind is considered too unlikely to justify reinforcing houses for high wind. High winds are dangerous also to small craft at sea. The Islands are natural locations for boating activities, but small craft have been caught at sea in

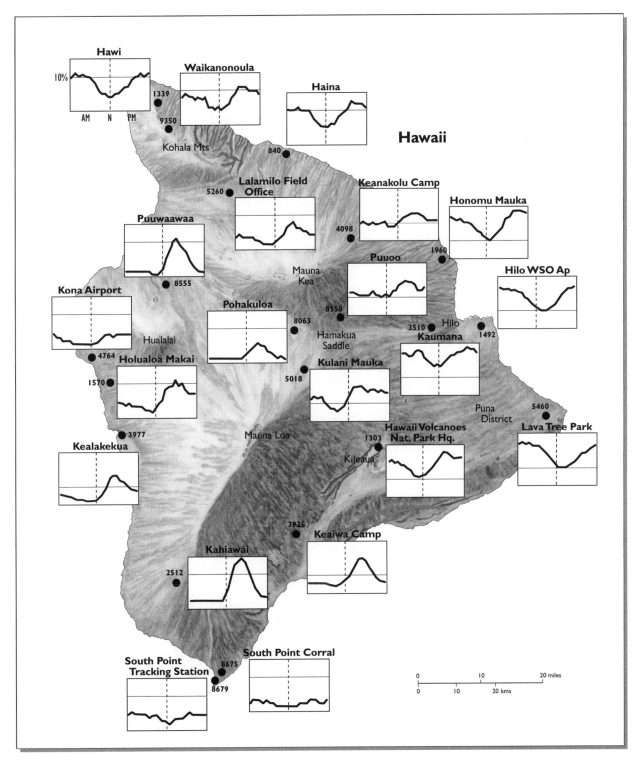

Figure 2.22 Diurnal rainfall variation on the island of Hawai'i from 24 National Weather Service rain gages 1962–1973 (after Schroeder et al., 1977)

deteriorating weather and occasionally boats have disappeared.

Hail and lightning are thunderstorm-produced phenomena that occur infrequently because thunderstorms are rare in Hawai'i (Table 2). The trade wind inversion generally restricts clouds from attaining the heights needed for thunderstorm development. A thunderstorm is reported if thunder is heard at a weather station. Thus the statistics represent limited areas near the major airport weather stations. It is thought that the Kona Coast of the Big Island and the slopes of Mauna Loa and Mauna Kea have more thunder than listed at the airport station, but these events are not recorded.

Lightning is a major weather hazard in the continental United States. Only recently have floods surpassed lightning as the number one weather-related killer. We know of no lightning-related fatalities in Hawai'i, although property is sometimes damaged. Persons engaged in water sports are at risk, as the high electrical conductivity of sea water allows a nearby strike to be a threat.

Hail has been known to occur on the high mountains. Though a rare event, hail has fallen at sea level in Hawai'i, and hailstones measuring 2.5 cm (1 in) in diameter have been reported on O'ahu.

A tornado is defined as a "violently rotating column of air pendant from a cumulonimbus cloud," and may have a visible condensation funnel. A waterspout has been defined as a tornado over water, but waterspouts are usually less intense than tornadoes. On the average, fourteen funnel clouds are reported in Hawai'i each year. Of these about six are waterspouts with surface water spray observed, and one may strike land as a tornado. The symbols in Figure 2.23 represent reported sightings; many others doubtless are unreported. One Hawaiian tornado has been filmed and analyzed. It moved on shore in Kailua Bay on the Kona Coast of the Big Island at midday on January 28, 1971. Fortunately only one minor injury occurred, although maximum wind speeds as the storm hit shore were estimated at approximately 200 km/hr (120 mph).

In Hawai'i, residents and visitors are often visually treated to two spectacular atmospheric phenomena: the rainbow and the green flash. Rainbows occur most frequently during the rainy season. Orographic showers along the windward slopes of the Islands produce morning rainbows, and afternoon showers over the central mountains such as the Ko'olau Range of O'ahu produce afternoon rainbows for viewers on the leeward sides. Rainbows are related to sunlight (for an explanation, see Chapter 3). The prevalence of rainbows in rainy Mānoa Valley, where the University of Hawaii campus is located, led to the popular nicknames of the University's athletic teams (Rainbow Warriors and Rainbow Wahines).

The green flash is elusive and less frequently observed, but rewarding to those who see it. This flash is a short-lived burst of green light seen as the sun's apparent disk sinks below (or rises above) a distant, clear horizon. It results from the scattering of sunlight by the atmosphere. The best time for observing a green flash is at sunset in winter, when the sun sets to the southwest and when calm, clear conditions are more frequent. A sunrise green flash is also possible, but favorable conditions for this phenomenon are less common.

Table 2 Annual Number of Thunderstorm Days for First-order Weather Stations in Hawai'i

Station (Island)	Number of Thunderstorm Days
Hilo (Hawai'i)	9
Kahului (Maui)	4
Honolulu (O'ahu)	7
Līhu'e (Kaua'i)	8

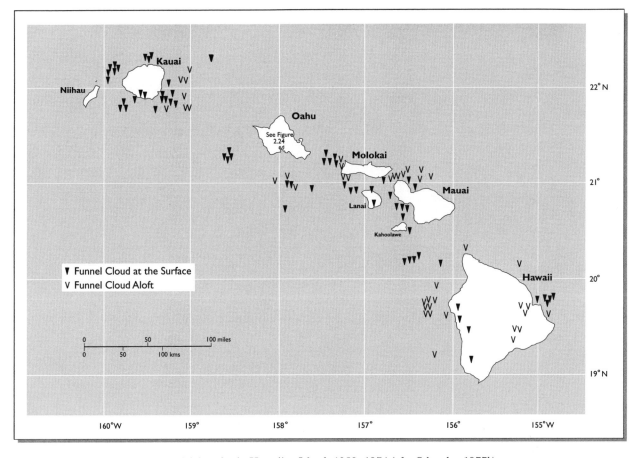

Figure 2.23 Waterspout and funnel sightings for the Hawaiian Islands 1959–1974 (after Schroeder, 1977b)

A Synthesis of the Climate Controls in the Islands

The interplay of large-scale weather systems with the topography of the individual islands produces a wide range of climates, and thus the term "climate by the mile" is often used in Hawai'i. Visitors will note that the flora and fauna of Hawai'i are as diverse as the localized micro-climates. We shall summarize our discussion of climate controls by examining highlights of the climate of each of the major islands, beginning in the northwest and proceeding southeast.

Kaua'i

Kaua'i consists primarily of one major eroded volcano, as described in Chapter 1. The prevailing trade winds move over the windward coast at Līhu'e, creating a relatively cool, moist climate in that region. The summit of Wai'ale'ale lies above a rampart facing the trades, so the orographic ascent of the trades produces prolonged rain at the cloud-shrouded summit. Kaua'i, the farthest north of the principal islands, also experiences the most winter storm and frontal activity. The central mass of

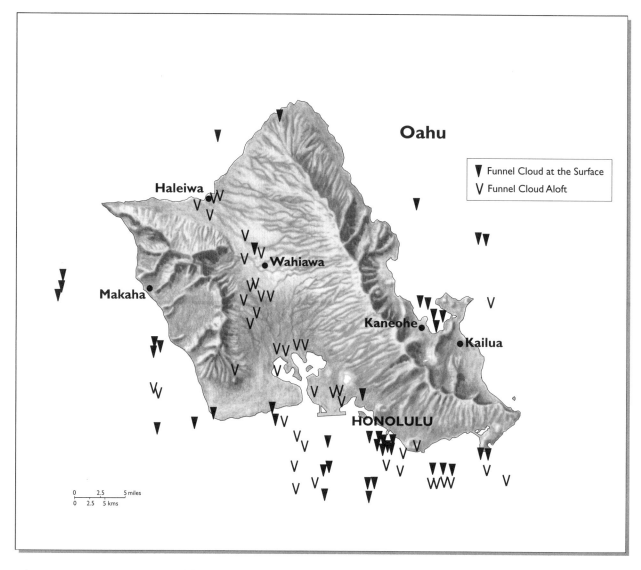

Figure 2.24 Waterspout and funnel sightings for Oʻahu

Waiʻaleʻale is shaped in such a way that orographic effects work for all wind exposures.

The western slopes of Kauaʻi are largely in the rain shadow of Waiʻaleʻale, so the climate is dry and desertlike. Here afternoon convection causes an afternoon rainfall maximum very different from the rainfall regime of the windward slopes. August max-

imum temperatures at leeward Mānā average 3 °C (5 °F) higher than in windward Līhuʻe because the moist, cloudy trade wind air mass carries cooler air and insulating clouds over Līhuʻe. The respective minimum temperatures, on the other hand, are nearly identical.

The prolonged periods of cloudiness at Waiʻale-

'ale have caused problems with maintenance of a summit rain gage. Historically, access was by a hike of several days from the leeward slope through a summit swampland. One hiker is known to have died on the trail. Currently, access to the gage is by helicopter. On a favorable day, a helicopter hovers overhead while the gage is read and the observer scrambles in and out before the weather deteriorates. Because there are long periods between gage readings, monthly statistics for Wai'ale'ale are poor, and the gage itself is nonstandard. A standard National Weather Service gage would overflow in a matter of days. Kaua'i is the wettest of all the Islands in rainfall, approximately 2,500 mm (100 in) per year, and as a result it has many perennial streams.

Ni'ihau

Little is known about the climate of Ni'ihau, since it has no weather station. It is privately owned and lightly populated. It is generally considered to be rather dry, rising as it does to only 390 m (1,281 ft), and lying in the rain shadow of Kaua'i.

O'ahu

O'ahu consists of the heavily eroded remnants of two volcanoes, Ko'olau and Wai'anae. The current Ko'olau Range is the western wall of a once-great shield volcano, while the Wai'anae Range is the eastern flank of a similar shield. The windward Ko'olau Range is much wetter than its sister range since it is aligned perpendicular to the trades, so orographic rains are common. The showers drift over the leeward slopes, typically in the evening and early morning hours. Rainfall maxima occur slightly to leeward of the actual crest. Mount Tantalus and the upper Mānoa valley are slightly wetter than the crest, while the wettest spot in the Ko'olaus, Kahana, is situated where the mountain range is broadest.

The Wai'anae Range is substantially drier than the Ko'olau Range. The rain shadow effect of the windward Ko'olau Range is easily noted by visual comparison of the cloud bases on each range from a vantage point in the center of the intervening land, the Wahiawā saddle. The leeward slopes of the Wai'anae Range suffer from a dry-season fire hazard. The Wai'anae Coast depends on winter rains and therefore has substantial interannual variability. One winter storm can provide half the annual rainfall.

Wind patterns are also distinct on O'ahu. The Ko'olau Pali is extremely windy and turbulent during trade wind days. The northern and southern tips of the Ko'olau Range (Kahuku and Koko Head) are wind-eroded since the trades funnel around the corners and accelerate. At Kahuku, wind energy farms have been developed, as we will see in Chapter 5. Occasionally, strong trades will gust through the leeward Ko'olau valleys. The windward valleys are actually rather calm, since the trades are slowed by the solid Ko'olau Range and must either ascend or be diverted around the barrier. The Wai'anae Coast between Wai'anae town and Nānākuli has a regular sea breeze. The leeward Wai'anae slopes have a distinct afternoon rainfall maximum similar to that of leeward Kaua'i.

Moloka'i

The island of Moloka'i, with its high eastern mass and a lower western elevation, is unique in the Islands in that it is aligned nearly parallel to the prevailing trades. A consequence of this is that the wind flow splits in passing East Moloka'i and the orographic lift is not as prominent as in the other islands. The northern coast of East Moloka'i is more efficient in orographically lifting northerly winds.

The northwestern portions of the island from Ho'olehua to 'Īlio Point are windswept, and Mo'omomi Beach is the site of the foremost wind-deposited sand dunes in the state. Although some preliminary wind-power exploration occurred here in the late 1970s, no development has followed. The western part of Moloka'i is dry. A convergence of trades diverted around the eastern mountain mass creates a cloud band which lies over the southern leeward coast and extends hundreds of kilometers downwind. This cloud band sometimes produces intense showers, called nāulu by the Hawaiians. These showers are noted for often falling just offshore during the summer drought.

Maui

As we noted in Chapter 1, Maui consists of two volcanic peaks: West Maui and Haleakalā. West Maui is an older and highly eroded volcano similar to Kaua'i, whereas Haleakalā is younger and still geologically active. (The last eruption was about 1790.) The climate of West Maui is similar to that of Wai'ale'ale, although Kukui, the summit, is more accessible than Wai'ale'ale and thus holds the official one-month rainfall record for the United States (2,717 mm/107 in). The leeward slopes of West Maui are dry. Lahaina resembles leeward Wai'anae on O'ahu and has a frequent sea breeze, though trades often occur to the north at Ka'anapali and south at Olowalu.

Haleakalā resembles Mauna Loa and Mauna Kea on the island of Hawai'i, as we will see in Chapter 4. The windward slopes are wet, and maximum rains fall along the slopes rather than at the summit as they do on West Maui, East Moloka'i, the Ko'olau Range, and Wai'ale'ale. Leeward slopes are dominated by circulations of sea or valley breezes. Transitions between these two climatic types occur along the northern and southern slopes.

The Haleakalā summit is a fascinating place to visit. The preferred time to arrive is immediately before sunrise. It is chilly, though not as cold as the higher Big Island peaks. The 3,055 m (10,023 ft) elevation is usually above the strongest trades and below the winter westerlies, although everything

changes during winter storm conditions. Ice has been recorded at 2,100 m (about 6,890 ft), and 1,270 mm (about 50 in) of rain fell in a three-day storm in January 1980. On a normal day, the sun rises above the trade wind clouds and its rays fill the large post-erosional caldera (the Crater). The primary summit is nearly 1,000 m (more than 3,000 ft) above the crater floor. The observer who stays beyond the sunrise may be treated to a wonderful weather show. Clouds will start to invade the crater as heating promotes upslope currents, which ascend through the interface between the inversion and the mountain. As the day continues, the clouds may completely surround the summit. Sometimes turrets may ascend above the summit in the surrounding air, leaving the visitor adrift in a sea of clouds. A visitor descending from the summit encounters chilly, damp, and sometimes drizzly weather, persisting to the cloud base well downslope.

A distinctive Maui feature is produced by interactions of trade winds with the two mountain masses. First filmed in the late 1940s by scientists with the Pineapple Research Institute, the feature has been dubbed the "Maui Vortex." Along the northern slopes of Haleakalā, the trade winds are diverted and accelerate through the central valley, making Kahului the windiest major airport in the state. The winds then encounter the West Maui mountain and are shunted to the south, through the harbor of Ma'alaea and over McGregor Point. The turning of the winds by topography appears as a more northerly wind at Kahului and as prevailing northerlies in Kihei, immediately south of Ma'alaea. Some effort has been made to harvest wind power in this region. One consequence of the acceleration of winds through the central valley is a divergence, or spreading out, of the surface layer of air. The resultant sinking air at higher elevations keeps Kahului dry, with an annual rainfall of less than 685 mm (27 in). The air diverted along the Kihei coast by the barrier effect of West Maui then ascends along the heated slopes of Haleakalā. The final picture, then, is air moving west along the north slope of Haleakalā, being deflected south upon encountering West Maui, then moving southeast up the west slope of Haleakalā. Cloud films taken from both West Maui and the Haleakalā slope above the inversion depict a spinning "vortex" along the northwest slope. The vortex has a clear "eye," which may be the source of the name Pukalani (literally "hole in the sky") of a village nearby. The vortex appears to play a significant role in recirculating air pollutants, such as smoke from agricultural fires, which normally would be expected to blow out to sea.

Lānaʻi

Lānaʻi lies in the rain shadow of Maui and is the driest populated island. It has one mountain peak, the summit of which is Lānaʻihale at 1,027 m (3,370 ft). Two interesting aspects of Lānaʻi's climate are worth discussion. A sea breeze develops to the lee of Lānaʻihale, and nāulu showers may occur along the sea-breeze front. The front often straddles the runway at the Lanai Airport. This leads to a situation in which a wind sock at the northeast end of the runway may indicate a northeast wind, while the sock at the southwest end may indicate a southwest wind.

Kahoʻolawe

Although Kahoʻolawe is unpopulated and appears desolate, anecdotal and archaeological evidence indicates that it once supported a Hawaiian population. The island was used as a ranch prior to the Second World War. It is commonly believed that the desolation is from degradation by feral goats, which drastically altered the native vegetation. Kahoʻolawe lies in the rain shadow of Haleakalā, but observations by one of the authors suggest that it has a unique source of rain. A cloud plume similar to the one formed over southwest Molokaʻi forms at the interface between the trades moving south of Haleakalā and the leeward sea breeze. This cloud is well-documented in weather satellite imagery. It often passes over Kahoʻolawe and has been observed producing showers both over the ocean between Kahoʻolawe and Haleakalā and over Kahoʻolawe.

Hawaiʻi

Hawaiʻi, the largest island, possesses the highest and most massive mountains. The island consists of the visible peaks of five volcanoes and includes buried remnants of two additional mountains. Each mountain as well as the integrated whole produces dramatic differences in climate, as will be explained in later chapters. Four significant rainfall maxima exist (see Chapter 4). The windward slopes of Mauna Loa and Mauna Kea are connected by the high Humuʻula Saddle, which effectively blocks most trade wind air. A continuous high rainfall belt extends from Kīlauea volcano eastward toward Cape Kumukahi, and northward along the slopes of Mauna Loa and Mauna Kea. At higher elevations rains diminish, and above the inversion desert climates appear. Although precipitation is difficult to measure at windswept mountain summits, estimates for Mauna Loa and Mauna Kea range between 355 and 406 mm (14–16 in)/yr. Most precipitation at these locations is frozen, falling as graupel (small soft hail) or snow. In favorable years people ski on Mauna Kea.

Another rainfall maximum occurs on the crest of the Kohala Mountain "range." Kohala is an extinct volcano which does not penetrate the inversion. Strong trades blow over Kohala, producing an orographic pattern with a distinct rain shadow. The trades over Kohala are diverted by Mauna Kea to the southeast and possibly by Haleakalā well to the northwest.

A unique rainfall regime occurs along the western

flank of Mauna Loa on the Kona Coast. Here, sea breezes converge with trade winds that have passed through the Humuʻula Saddle and over the upper slopes of Mauna Loa. Showers develop in the afternoon and drift toward the shores at night. By morning, the slopes are clear and the process begins anew. This regime is common during the summer trade wind season. Kona is unique in the state in having a summer rainfall maximum.

The Kona Coast rainfall belt extends to Hualālai, a volcano which is considered still active (it last erupted in 1801). Its summit is near the inversion. There are two weather regimes. The southern- and western-facing slopes share the summer showers of the Mauna Loa portion of Kona, while the northern and eastern slopes have irregular convective showers. The area between Mauna Loa and Hualālai has little weather information.

A drive around the Big Island provides an opportunity to view a natural climate laboratory. If the drivers have access to the high mountains, they can pass through four climatic regimes in a single day. Between Honokaʻa and Waimea one drives from tropical rain forests through temperate pine forests to arid rangeland with cactus, while driving through Hawaii Volcanoes National Park one passes through rain forest and lava desert. A drive (in violation of rental car contracts) into the Humuʻula Saddle affords the opportunity to climb above the inversion. From a vantage point on the roads to either Mauna Kea or Mauna Loa, one can observe trade clouds and sea-breeze clouds facing each other across the saddle.

This chapter has attempted to describe the chief large-scale and meso-climate controls in the Hawaiian Islands, and to identify some interesting aspects of the resulting climate. Certainly the predominant trade winds, and the ways they interact with the variable topography of the Islands, are the chief reason for the wide range of climates. Frequent interruptions of the prevailing trade wind conditions, however, add even greater variability to the picture. Details of the rainfall climatology of the Islands can be found in Chapter 4.

SUGGESTED READINGS

Blumenstock, D. I., and Price, S. 1967. "The climate of Hawaii." In *Climates of the states* (volume II: Western States), 614–639. Port Washington, New York: Water Information Center, Inc.

Houghton, D., and Sanders, F. 1988. *Weather at sea.* Camden, Maine: International Marine Publishing Co., 197 pp.

Price, S. 1973. "Climate." In *Atlas of Hawaii,* 53–60. Honolulu: University of Hawaii Press.

Ramage, C. S. 1962. The subtropical cyclone. *Journal Geophysical Research* 67:1401–1411.

Simpson, R. H. 1952. Evaluation of the Kona storm: A subtropical cyclone. *Journal Meteorology* 9 (1): 24–35.

CHAPTER 3

Radiation and Energy Balances and Air Temperature

Dennis Nullet and Marie Sanderson

Introduction

The sun provides as much energy to the earth in one minute as humans currently generate artificially in an entire year. This energy, in the form of solar radiation (sunshine), may change form many times in the earth-atmosphere system before eventually returning to space. During its residence on earth, the energy given us by the sun may accomplish many tasks, from feeding plants to driving hurricanes. In fact, virtually all climatic and life processes on earth depend directly or indirectly on solar radiation as an energy source.

One approach scientists use to understand these processes is to track the path of this energy as it is converted from one form to another. The concept of an environmental balance provides a useful tool for this task. Since energy can neither be created nor destroyed, but can change form, the energy entering a system must equal the energy leaving the system plus the change in energy storage.

This chapter discusses the balance of energy entering and leaving the surface of the earth in Hawai'i. The discussion begins by exploring the radiation balance, a component of the complete energy balance that has attracted a good deal of research in Hawai'i. The radiation balance tallies radiant energy from the sun, earth, and sky. The major source of energy to the surface, solar radiation, is considered in greatest depth.

The Radiation Balance

Radiant energy from the sun travels at the speed of light in the form of electromagnetic waves with characteristic wavelengths. The complete range of radiation wavelengths, known as the electromagnetic spectrum, is often grouped into familiar bands such as visible light, X-rays, and radio waves.

All matter emits radiant energy. The amount of radiation given off by a surface increases exponentially with its absolute (Kelvin) temperature ($0\,°K$ is

–273 °C). The sun has a surface temperature of approximately 6,000° Kelvin and radiates primarily in the ultraviolet (9%), visible (45%), and infrared (46%) regions of the spectrum. Sunlight has a maximum intensity at about 0.50 micrometers (μm) in the green band of visible light. Climatologists call radiation emitted by the sun shortwave radiation, solar radiation, or insolation. The earth has an average surface temperature of about 288° Kelvin (15° C), and it radiates in the far-infrared region with a maximum intensity at about 9.7 μm. Radiation emitted by the earth's surface and atmosphere is called longwave, or terrestrial, radiation. Figure 3.1 illustrates the solar and terrestrial radiation spectra.

Radiation is commonly measured in calories per square centimeter (cal/cm²). A calorie is the amount of energy required to raise one gram of water one degree centigrade at a temperature of fifteen degrees centigrade. Scientists also use the units watts and joules to describe radiation. A watt is a measure of the intensity of radiation, while joules describe the total radiant energy received over a given period of time. One joule equals 0.239 calories, and a watt is one joule per second.

The radiation balance simply accounts for the fluxes in radiation at all wavelengths toward and away from a surface. The accounting equation can be written,

$$Q_* = Q\!\downarrow - Q\!\uparrow + L\!\downarrow - L\!\uparrow$$

where Q_* is net allwave radiation, $Q\!\downarrow$ is insolation or solar radiation, $Q\!\uparrow$ is reflected solar radiation, $L\!\downarrow$ is incoming longwave radiation, and $L\!\uparrow$ is longwave radiation emitted and reflected by the surface. These quantities and their measurement in Hawai'i are discussed in detail below.

Solar Radiation (Insolation)

The distribution of average annual solar radiation (insolation) at the surface of the major Hawaiian Islands is shown in Figure 3.2. These maps were compiled by the Department of Land and Natural Resources based on available insolation measurements. Most of the data, from nearly 100 stations, has been compiled by local sugar companies, because cane yields are directly related to insolation. Consequently, most measurements are made in lowland agricultural areas. The sugar companies' standard field instrument, the "wigwag," activates a counter as two sensors rock back and forth in response to vapor-pressure changes in alcohol when exposed to sunlight. Before 1969, photochemical tubes, containing a chemical that decomposes when exposed to insolation, were common.

Several scientific projects in Hawai'i, measuring radiation with high quality pyranometers, have studied solar radiation in urban areas to evaluate the potential for solar energy development. Data for higher elevations are sparse, although important instrument transects have been made on Mauna Loa, Mauna Kea, Haleakalā, and the Ko'olau Range on O'ahu. The longest-running mountain station has been the Mauna Loa Observatory (MLO), which provides baseline radiation data for researchers worldwide. In addition to the insolation measurements, hours-of-bright-sunshine records have been kept at the major airports by the National Weather Service, and at various agricultural locations. The percentage-of-possible-sunshine record for Honolulu is longest, going back to 1905. Prior to 1946, the instruments were atop the old Federal Building and on the roof of the former Alexander Young Hotel in downtown Honolulu. After 1946, instruments were shifted to the Honolulu Airport. Historical trends in insolation for Hawai'i are discussed in Chapter 6.

Large gradients characterize most aspects of the climate of Hawai'i, and as Figure 3.2 shows, insolation is no exception. To understand the patterns, the celestial and atmospheric controls on insolation, and

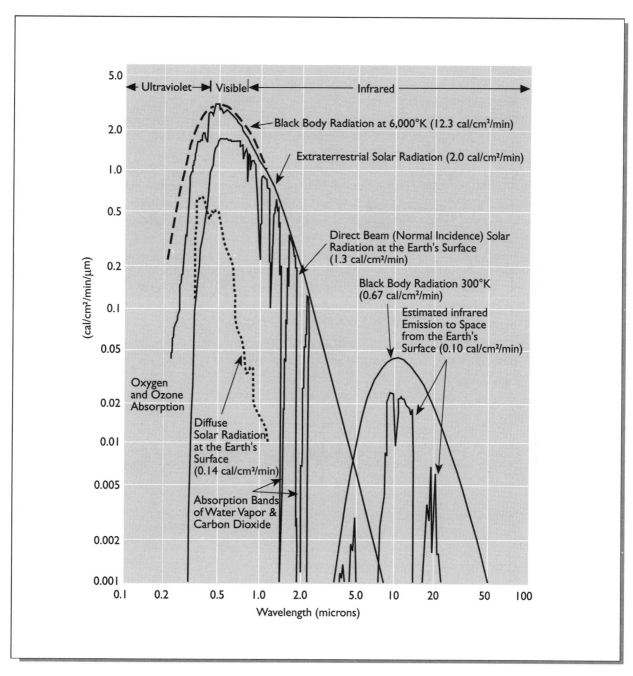

Figure 3.1 Electromagnetic spectra of solar and terrestrial radiation (adapted with permission from Sellers, 1965)

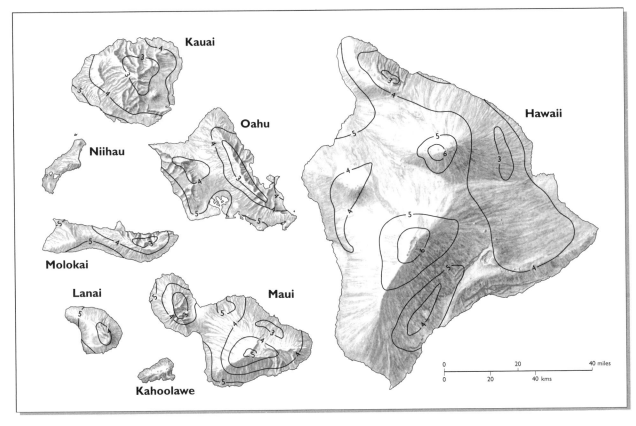

Figure 3.2 Average annual global radiation (hundreds of cal/cm²/day) (Niʻihau and Kahoʻolawe, no data)

the way in which the Islands themselves modify the radiation environment, must be considered.

Extraterrestrial Radiation

Radiation from the sun arriving at the outer limits of the earth's atmosphere is called extraterrestrial radiation. The intensity of this radiation depends on the radiant output of the sun, the distance of the earth from the sun, and the latitude at which radiation is being measured. The average value of the intensity of extraterrestrial radiation, often called the solar constant, is about 1.96 cal/cm²/minute. Despite the implications of the term solar constant, some scientists theorize that changes in the intensity of extraterrestrial radiation reaching the earth may be responsible for past climatic changes, such as the initiation of ice ages.

While the earth's orbital characteristics and the Islands' latitude determine the intensity of solar radiation in the atmosphere above the Islands, they also determine the daily path of the sun across the sky in Hawaiʻi. The position of the sun in the sky and the length of the day throughout the year at Honolulu are summarized in a sky chart (Figure 3.3). The sun's position is described by the solar elevation (concentric circles) and an azimuth (radial lines). The path of the sun through the sky (curved lines oriented right to left) is shown for several celes-

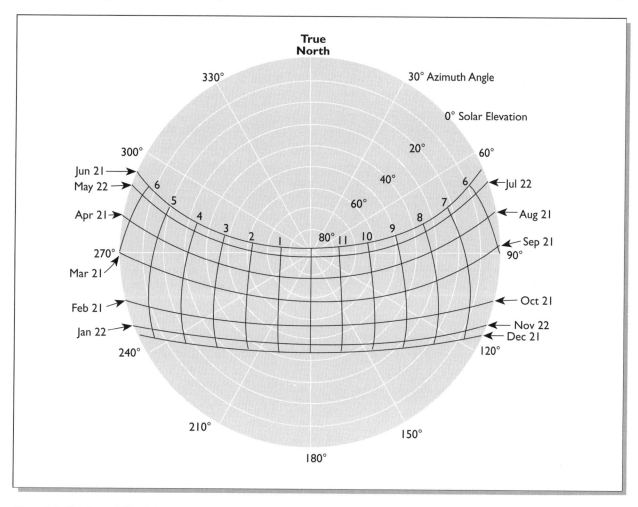

Figure 3.3 Sky chart of Honolulu, Hawai'i (adapted from Yoshihara and Eilern, 1987)

tially important dates of the year. The vertical curved lines show the time of day. In Hawai'i, the shortest day of the year, the winter solstice, when the sun is directly over the Tropic of Capricorn in the Southern Hemisphere is December 21, and it is 10 hours and 50 minutes long. The longest day of the year, the summer solstice, when the sun is directly over the Tropic of Cancer, is June 21, is 13 hours and 20 minutes long. In both hemispheres in summer, higher latitudes (where the days are longer)

may actually receive more total—though less intense —insolation than Hawai'i. (In fact, the highest extraterrestrial one-day insolation total on the planet is found at the South Pole on December 21.) Of course, the situation is reversed in winter; Hawai'i's nights seem short compared to the protracted nights of higher latitudes.

Hawai'i is the only place in the United States where the noonday sun is directly overhead twice a year, on approximately May 27 and July 17. On these days, vertical surfaces cast no shadows at solar noon. Between these dates the sun lies to the north of the zenith in Hawai'i. By contrast, in New York City (41°N), the noonday sun reaches only 72.5° above the horizon at the summer solstice. At the winter solstice, the Hawaiian noon sun (at Honolulu's latitude) still rises to an altitude of 45°, while in New York it clears the horizon by only 25.5°.

The intensity of radiation produced by the sun, the distance between the earth and sun, the length of day, the altitude of the sun in the sky, and the manner in which these parameters change through the year determine the quantity of radiation that will fall on a level surface of the earth in the absence of an atmosphere. This quantity is commonly called Angot's value, after the turn-of-the-century French meteorologist, Charles Alfred Angot. Angot's values of total daily radiation (using a solar constant of 1.96 cal/cm²/min) for Honolulu's latitude are compared with three other major cities in Figure 3.4. Even though summer radiation totals at the high-latitude cities exceed Honolulu's because of longer days, the

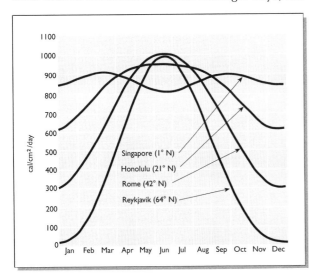

Figure 3.4 Angot values for four selected world stations (cal/cm²/day)

midday radiation intensity is still higher in Hawai'i. This means that while a person is more likely to get a bad sunburn in summer in Honolulu, bigger vegetables can probably be grown in summer in Reykjavik, Iceland, because of the length of daylight.

Effects of the Atmosphere on Solar Radiation

At the end of its journey from the sun to the earth's surface, solar radiation must pass through the earth's atmosphere. Here, it interacts with gas molecules, suspended particles, and clouds in a variety of ways.

The atmosphere scatters solar radiation, changing its direction when the solar ray impinges on an air molecule or particle. The smallest particles selectively scatter short wavelengths, such as blue light, causing the sky to appear blue in daylight. This selective scattering also causes sunlight, depleted of its blue color, to appear red at sunset. Larger particles, such as sea salt and volcanic dust, scatter all wavelengths equally and make the sky appear hazy, or white. Eruptions of volcanoes on the Big Island can reduce visibility to less than a mile, producing a haze residents call "vog." Generally, a good rain will wash most volcanic particles out of the lower atmosphere and restore the clarity of the air and the characteristic deep blue skies of Hawai'i.

The atmosphere also absorbs some solar radiation. Ozone is particularly important because it strongly absorbs ultraviolet light (UV), which can cause cell damage in plants and animals. The amount of UV in the solar spectrum is reduced by the atmosphere to only about 4 to 5% of the total energy in solar radiation measured at the surface, while it constitutes 9% of extraterrestrial radiation. Generally, there is considerably less ozone in the atmosphere above Hawai'i than at mid-latitude locations; for example, 25% less than over the U.S.–Canada border. This difference is one reason that UV is more intense in Hawai'i than at higher latitudes. Water vapor is another strong absorber of solar radiation. In Hawai'i, if all the water in the atmosphere suddenly rained out, it would form a layer between 25 and 35 mm (1 and 1.4 in) deep on average. This is enough to absorb about 14% of insolation, mostly at infrared wavelengths. As most of the atmospheric water vapor is concentrated near sea level, absorption of solar radiation by water vapor decreases with elevation.

The atmosphere also acts as a lens to bend, or refract, solar radiation. Refraction can separate the colors in the solar beam to produce optical effects such as the green flash at sunset and the Islands' ubiquitous rainbows. Rainbows form only when the sun shines on raindrops. If you stand facing the rainbow, the sun will always be behind you with your shadow pointing toward the rainy center of the arch. The short wavelength colors, violet and blue, appear on the inside of the rainbow, and the long wavelength colors, red and orange, on the outside. This pattern reverses if there is a secondary rainbow.

Finally, the atmosphere—especially clouds in the atmosphere—can also reflect some of the incoming solar radiation. The combined optical effects of the atmosphere both reduce the intensity and change the character of solar radiation measured at the surface. Radiation that has been scattered or reflected and approaches the earth from other than the direction of the sun is called diffuse or sky radiation. Radiation that reaches the surface from the direction of the sun is termed direct-beam radiation, and the sum of direct-beam and diffuse radiation is called global radiation, or insolation.

Diffuse radiation may account for 100% of the insolation measured on a densely overcast day in Hawai'i. At the Holmes Hall station of the University of Hawaii campus, measurements have shown that diffuse radiation accounts for 37% of insolation for all days, 15% on the clearest days, and 77% on the mostly cloudy days. Diffuse radiation is generally unsuitable for solar energy applications, as it is difficult to focus. On the other hand, a high ratio of diffuse to direct-beam radiation is beneficial to plants, because diffuse radiation has a high visible-light content as a result of selective scattering and greater canopy penetration.

Influence of the Islands on Solar Radiation Received

The extraterrestrial radiation cycle and the optical properties of the atmosphere determine the total amount of solar radiation (insolation) that reaches the earth's surface on a clear day. Insolation also depends on the distribution of clouds and on the slope, aspect, and elevation of the surface.

The highest radiation totals are recorded on clear days. Less radiation is recorded on days in which clouds block the sun. In Hawai'i, completely cloudless days are extremely rare. For example, in eleven years of pyranometer data recorded at the University of Hawaii (1976 to 1987), there were fewer than ten completely clear days. The principal cause of the spatial variation in annual global radiation seen in Figure 3.2 is variable daytime cloud cover. At windward sites, the trade winds push air up the slopes and orographic clouds form. Here insolation is least. An exception is the windward shore of Lāna'i, which lies in the rain shadow of West Maui. Because of its association with cloudiness, the rainfall distribution, which will be seen in Chapter 4, is inversely related to the insolation pattern. Dry leeward sites receive the most insolation. This pattern is interrupted on the leeward Big Island, where afternoon sea breezes bring clouds to the lee slopes of Mauna Kea, Mauna Loa, and Hualālai. The effect of the trade wind inversion is evident on the mountains of Haleakalā, Mauna Kea, and Mauna Loa. As the temperature inversion suppresses vertical cloud development, the high mountains experience more clear skies (50% of the time at MLO), and thus also the highest insolation totals (up to 700 cal/cm² per day).

The orographic cloud remains relatively stationary along the mountain slopes. This persistence produces dramatic gradients in the average insolation. The clouds also act as stationary reflectors and increase diffuse radiation at nearby sites. Because of cloud reflection, radiation intensities measured at the head of Mānoa Valley near Honolulu have occasionally exceeded the solar constant. In winter, when the sun is low in the southern sky, the sun's rays are able to penetrate beneath the orographic cloud cap. This helps explain the curious observation that insolation on the southern flank of Mauna Loa shows little annual variation.

At the University of Hawaii at Mānoa on leeward Oʻahu, insolation for the period 1979–1981 averaged 81% of the clear-sky value in January and 82% in July, the reduction caused by clouds. In contrast, for the same time period at Maunawili, on windward Oʻahu, insolation averaged 58% of clear-day radiation in January and only 50% in July. Maunawili lies under a persistent orographic cloud cap produced when the trade winds encounter the Koʻolau Range. The effect of clouds on insolation received at these two locations is illustrated in Figure 3.5. Notice that cloudiness at Maunawili increases both the magnitude of diffuse radiation and the percentage of insolation that arrives as diffuse radiation.

Slope, aspect, and elevation also influence the insolation. Slopes that face the sun receive more radiation than slopes that face away from the sun. As at higher latitudes, this effect is particularly pronounced in winter in Hawaiʻi, when the sun remains relatively low in the sky. For example, under clear skies in December, a 30° south-facing slope receives around 650 cal/cm²/day, while a 30° north-

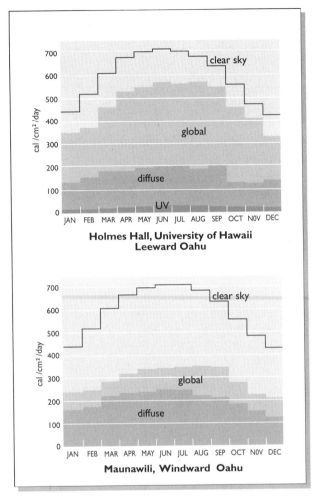

Figure 3.5 The effect of clouds on solar radiation on leeward and windward Oʻahu

facing slope receives only 175 cal/cm²/day. On slopes with a diurnal variation in cloudiness, the daily path of the sun in the sky can be important. An example is the west-facing, leeward side of the Big Island. In the morning when skies are clear, insolation is low because the slopes face away from the sun. In the afternoon, sea-breeze clouds form and obscure the sun in what would normally be the high sun period of the day. This cycle is utilized by local

Kona coffee growers who depend on the afternoon cloud buildup to regulate the intensity of insolation. Shadows can be important when the terrain is exceptionally steep. For example, in December, insolation at the Maunawili station at the base of the northeast-facing Pali cliffs in Oʻahu was 40% below coastal sites, while measured radiation at Lyon Arboretum, on the lee side facing southwest, was only 10% below coastal sites.

On clear days, insolation increases with elevation as the air mass that solar radiation must penetrate decreases. The combined effects of atmospheric attenuation, cloudiness, and elevation are illustrated in Table 3, which compares extraterrestrial, clear-day, and average-day insolation at Honolulu at sea level, and at MLO at 3,400 m (11,200 ft). The extraterrestrial values were computed from known formulae, clear-day values were estimated using a parameterization model called SPCTRAL2, and the average-day values are monthly averages measured by Eppley pyranometers. Because of the reduced optical path and clean skies above MLO, clear-day insolation there averages 82% of the annual extra-terrestrial value, compared to 73% at sea level. Also, the percent attenuation by clouds (compare the clear- and average-day values) is higher at sea level than at high elevations.

The distribution of average insolation in cal/cm²/ hr at different times of year is shown in Figure 3.6. Annual variation is rather small, in contrast to high latitudes. This pattern results primarily from the annual variation in extraterrestrial radiation. At Honolulu there tends to be more cloud attenuation

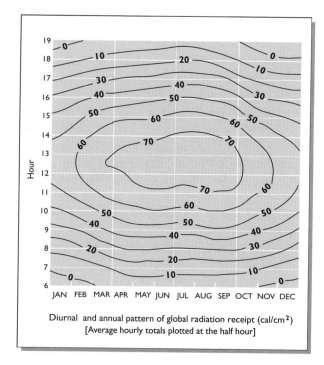

Diurnal and annual pattern of global radiation receipt (cal/cm²)
[Average hourly totals plotted at the half hour]

Figure 3.6 Diurnal and monthly patterns of global radiation for Honolulu (cal/cm²/hr)

Table 3 Average Monthly Solar Radiation (cal/cm²/day)

	Jan	Feb	Mar	Apr	May	Jun	Jul	Aug	Sep	Oct	Nov	Dec	Ann
Honolulu, sea level													
Extraterrestrial	642	731	832	906	939	946	939	914	857	765	667	614	813
Clear day	446	521	607	671	701	707	702	680	630	551	468	423	592
Average (1932–1985)	366	428	487	539	576	594	594	585	551	468	389	351	494
MLO, 3,400 meters													
Extraterrestrial	667	754	843	905	919	913	907	896	853	771	678	635	813
Clear day	525	602	688	750	775	780	775	756	709	632	547	501	670
Average (1958–1972 and 1978–1983)	507	564	589	616	656	717	694	650	610	542	487	468	592

in the morning than in the afternoon, and it is cloudier in spring than in fall.

Terrestrial Radiation

The earth and atmosphere as a whole emit radiation to space at the same rate that radiation from the sun is absorbed. If this were not the case, the earth's surface would be either heating or cooling. Terrestrial radiation to space is concentrated in a few wavelength bands, as was seen in Figure 3.1, based on the radiative absorption properties of atmospheric gases. Several of these gases are transparent to short wavelengths, such as visible light, but strongly absorb longer wavelengths. Thus, the atmosphere easily admits solar radiation but grudgingly releases the longwave terrestrial radiation emitted by the earth's surface. As a result, the earth's atmosphere acts as a blanket, warming the surface by trapping solar energy. This has been called the "greenhouse effect." In the absence of an atmosphere, the average surface temperature would be nearly $-20\,°C$ ($-4\,°F$) rather than the current $15\,°C$ ($59\,°F$). This represents a small temperature difference as planetary surfaces go, but it has had tremendous implications for the development of life on earth, for it means the difference between frozen and liquid water at the surface. The greenhouse effect is further discussed in Chapter 7.

The pattern and character of terrestrial radiation depend on the temperature of exposed surfaces, the atmospheric composition profile, and the presence of clouds. In Hawai'i, temperatures at the earth's surface range from below freezing in the high mountains to $35\,°C$ ($95\,°F$) in dry leeward areas. At $0\,°C$ ($32\,°F$), an ideal surface radiates about 0.46 cal/cm²/min, and at $35\,°C$ ($95\,°F$), about 0.74 cal/cm²/min. Unlike solar radiation, terrestrial radiation continues through the night. The diurnal range can be quite large at the upper slopes of the high mountains, with high daytime temperatures and low nighttime temperatures, or relatively constant at the cloudy head of deep valleys near sea level.

The atmosphere also radiates. Atmospheric radiation depends primarily on temperature, water vapor, carbon dioxide, and clouds and is directed both upward and downward. Some of this radiation is lost to space, some is reabsorbed in the atmosphere, and some is returned to earth as counterradiation. The net longwave radiation lost from a surface is the amount radiated by the surface minus the amount counterradiated by the atmosphere. When clouds obscure the sky, counterradiation is much greater than under clear skies, and thus the net longwave loss is lower. Over the ocean off Barbers Point, O'ahu, the net longwave radiation loss has been measured as 0.12 cal/cm²/min under clear skies and only 0.04 cal/cm²/min under cloudy skies. These values correspond to 18% and 6% respectively of the total longwave radiation emitted by the ocean surface. Over sugar cane and pineapple, the net longwave radiation loss has been measured as 0.11 cal/cm²/min, and at MLO over bare lava, 0.22 cal/cm²/min under clear skies. All of these were nighttime measurements.

Topography also helps determine net longwave losses. Valley walls and other obstructions counterradiate at approximately the same intensity as outgoing longwave radiation. This reduces the net longwave radiation loss from that observed if all the counterradiation is from open sky. For example, net longwave radiation measurements at the head of Mānoa Valley in November and December of 1981 under clear skies were 0.057 and 0.066 cal/cm²/min, while net longwave radiation at a neighboring ridge site (unobstructed) was 0.086 to 0.089 cal/cm²/min.

Net Radiation

The difference between the quantity of radiation arriving at and leaving a surface determines the net gain or loss of radiant energy for the surface.

This quantity is called net allwave radiation, or simply net radiation, as defined by the equation on page 38. The percentage of insolation reflected, called the surface albedo, depends on the physical characteristics of the surface and the incidence angle and wavelength of the solar ray. In general, the higher the solar altitude, the lower the surface albedo. In Hawai'i, albedos tend to be slightly lower than for similar surfaces at higher latitudes. The albedo of a surface can vary with the wavelength. For example, plants reflect a much higher percentage of near-infrared radiation than visible light. An extreme case is pineapple leaves, which reflect less than 10% of visible light, but 55% to 75% of the energy in wavelengths between 0.7 μm and 1.25 μm. Soils tend to reflect radiation more uniformly at all wavelengths. In general, an increase in wetness means a decrease in albedo. As a result, the albedo tends to be lower for rainy and irrigated areas than dry areas. The albedo of bare soil ranges from 10% for dark, wet soils and lava rock to 30% for beach sand. The albedo of irrigated sugar cane is about 15%.

A rule of thumb is that at sea level in Hawai'i, net radiation equals about two-thirds of insolation over pineapple, grass sod, and sugar cane. The ratio of net radiation to insolation is generally higher than that measured at higher latitudes, mostly because of lower albedo values in Hawai'i. At MLO, net radiation over lava rock has been measured as 50% of insolation on a clear day in June and 41% on a clear day in December. High longwave radiation losses into the dry atmosphere and generally clear skies above MLO are responsible for this low fraction.

The distribution of average annual net radiation over the Islands is shown in Figure 3.7. These maps are based on both net radiation measurements and estimates of net radiation by empirical formulae, incorporating insolation, air temperature, and cloudiness estimates. Because of the paucity of net radiation data and questionable validity of the estimating model, the maps should be regarded as indicating a pattern, rather than showing the absolute magnitude of net radiation.

The net radiation pattern echoes the incoming solar radiation pattern below the trade wind inversion. The high net longwave radiation loss above the inversion offsets high incoming solar radiation values, and net radiation at these elevations remains fairly stable (approximately 300 cal/cm²/day). Cloud cover has a stabilizing influence on net radiation. On nearly cloudless days, insolation is high, but net longwave loss is also high. With greater cloudiness, insolation is low but most of it is retained as net radiation because the net longwave radiation loss is also low. As a result, average annual net radiation varies little from place to place over the Islands. In fact, about half of the combined land area of the major Islands receives between 250 and 300 cal/cm²/day as an annual average. The highest net radiation values are found on the dry leeward coasts of the Islands, and the lowest values are found along the wet windward slopes.

The Energy Balance

The radiation balance provides an estimate of net radiation, the principal source of energy to the surface. The partitioning of this energy into other forms is enumerated in the complete energy balance as follows:

$$Q. + A = LE + H + G + P$$

where Q. is net radiation, A is advected (horizontally moving) energy, LE is latent heat absorbed in evaporation, H is the heat flux to the air, G is the heat flux to the ground, and P is energy consumed in photosynthesis.

On a daily basis, the net heat flux into the ground is usually considered to be negligible; the amount of heat the surface sends downward during the day is equal to the heat released at night. Photosynthesis is

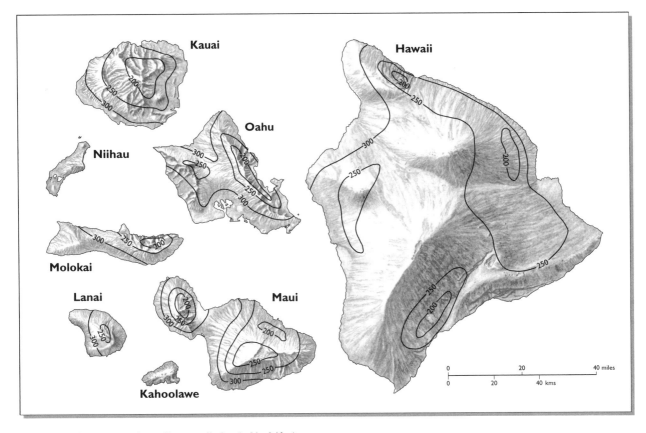

Figure 3.7 Average annual net allwave radiation (cal/cm²/day)

generally negligible as well, absorbing only about 1% of net radiation, most of this in the visible light range. Of the above terms, therefore, evaporation and heating of the air are the major sinks for the energy sources of net radiation and advection. These terms are so dominant that the ratio of H to LE, often called the Bowen ratio, has been used in classifying climate.

Advection, the horizontal transport of energy, usually in the form of sensible heat (heat which can be felt, or sensed), is quite important in the Hawaiian Islands. It is through advection that the surrounding ocean influences air temperatures over the Islands. After all, the Hawaiian Islands are at the same latitude as the Sahara Desert. In the absence of advection, the Islands would be hotter both during the day and in summer and cooler both at night and in winter. Advection from the ocean can be either positive (warming the air) or negative (cooling the air). A study of pan evaporation and solar radiation data at windward sites in Hawai'i has indicated that oceanic advection ranges from 49 cal/cm²/day in November to –42 cal/cm²/day in June. Advection from land sources can also be a source of considerable energy in drier areas of the Islands, originating over hot, exposed land such as lava flows and bare fields. In the Maui Saddle region, for example, advection from land sources has been estimated at approximately 164 cal/cm²/day in June. This kind of energy is not always welcome. Energy advected over an irrigated sugarcane field can increase transpiration and thus the amount of water needed to irrigate the crop.

As discussed above, most of the available net radiation is converted to sensible or latent heat. Sensible heat is measured by thermometers recording temperature, and latent heat is absorbed when water changes to its vapor phase through evaporation. The air temperatures in Hawai'i are discussed below, and information on evaporation and transpiration can be found in Chapter 4.

Air Temperatures in Hawai'i

The temperature of the air is the climatic parameter that is probably of most interest to residents and visitors to Hawai'i. This element is the combined result of the factors we have discussed earlier: the radiation and energy balances, the topography of the Islands, and cooling or warming by advection.

Air temperatures throughout the world are usually measured in a louvered housing called a Stevenson screen at a height of 1.5 m (5 ft) above the ground. This elevation has been agreed upon by the World Meteorological Organization (WMO) as the proper height to minimize the effect on air temperature of the earth's surface itself, where the radiative exchanges described earlier take place. At a standard weather station, a maximum and minimum thermometer are mounted in the screen and read twice daily (Figure 3.8). The mean daily temperature is approximated by the average of the maximum and minimum readings for the day. In the United States, weather data are gathered and disseminated by the National Oceanographic and Atmospheric Administration (NOAA).

The WMO has established a standard period of thirty years over which "mean" or "normal" cli-

Figure 3.8 Stevenson screen (a) and maximum and minimum thermometers (b)

mate data are computed, and the most recent temperature normals are for the period 1961–1990. Table 4 lists the maximum, minimum, and mean temperatures as well as monthly precipitation means for several representative stations in Hawai'i: Honolulu (O'ahu), Līhu'e (Kaua'i), Lahaina and

Table 4 Average Climatic Data for Seven Hawaiian Stations (1961–1990)

Honolulu (Oʻahu)

		Jan	Feb	Mar	Apr	May	June	July	Aug	Sept	Oct	Nov	Dec	Year
Max	T °F	80.1	80.5	81.6	82.8	84.7	86.5	87.5	88.7	88.5	86.9	84.1	81.2	84.4
	T °C	26.7	26.9	27.6	28.2	29.3	30.3	30.8	31.5	31.4	30.5	28.9	27.3	29.1
Min	T °F	65.4	65.4	67.2	68.1	70.3	72.2	73.4	74.0	73.5	72.3	70.3	67.0	70.0
	T °C	18.6	18.6	19.6	20.1	21.3	22.3	23.0	23.4	23.1	22.4	21.3	19.4	21.1
Mn	T °F	72.4	72.0	74.4	75.3	77.5	79.4	80.5	81.4	81.0	79.6	77.2	74.1	77.2
	T °C	22.4	22.2	23.6	24.1	25.3	26.3	26.9	27.4	27.2	26.4	25.1	23.4	25.1
P	(in)	3.55	2.21	22.0	1.54	1.13	0.50	0.59	0.44	0.78	2.28	3.00	3.80	22.02
	(mm)	90	56	56	39	29	13	15	11	20	58	76	97	560

Lahaina (Maui)

		Jan	Feb	Mar	Apr	May	June	July	Aug	Sept	Oct	Nov	Dec	Year
Max	T °F	81.8	81.9	82.9	83.5	85.1	86.6	87.6	88.4	88.6	87.7	85.6	82.0	85.2
	T °C	27.7	27.7	28.3	28.6	29.4	30.3	30.9	31.3	31.4	30.9	29.8	27.8	29.6
Min	T °F	63.7	63.1	64.5	64.2	66.8	68.0	69.1	69.7	69.6	68.7	67.1	64.8	66.7
	T °C	17.6	17.3	18.1	17.9	19.3	20.0	20.6	20.9	20.9	20.4	19.5	18.2	19.3
Mn	T °F	72.8	72.6	73.5	74.6	76.0	77.3	78.3	79.1	79.1	78.2	76.3	73.4	76.0
	T °C	22.7	22.6	23.1	23.7	24.4	25.2	25.7	26.2	26.2	25.7	24.6	23.0	24.4
P	(in)	3.49	2.35	1.79	1.05	0.61	0.09	0.17	0.18	0.34	1.09	2.15	3.20	16.51
	(mm)	89	60	45	27	15	2	4	5	9	28	55	81	420

Līhuʻe (Kauaʻi)

		Jan	Feb	Mar	Apr	May	June	July	Aug	Sept	Oct	Nov	Dec	Year
Max	T °F	77.9	78.1	78.5	79.6	81.2	82.1	84.1	84.8	84.8	83.3	80.7	78.6	81.2
	T °C	25.5	25.6	25.8	26.4	27.3	27.8	28.9	29.3	29.3	28.5	27.1	25.9	27.3
Min	T °F	65.3	65.1	66.9	68.5	70.3	72.5	73.7	74.2	73.5	72.0	70.3	67.1	70.0
	T °C	18.5	18.4	19.4	20.3	21.3	22.5	23.2	23.4	23.1	22.2	21.3	19.5	21.1
Mn	T °F	71.6	71.6	72.7	74.0	75.8	77.8	78.9	79.5	79.2	77.6	75.5	72.9	75.6
	T °C	22.0	22.0	22.6	23.3	24.3	25.4	26.1	26.4	26.2	25.3	24.2	22.7	24.2
P	(in)	5.89	3.33	4.17	3.50	3.15	1.65	2.17	1.76	2.37	4.41	5.45	5.15	43.00
	(mm)	150	85	106	89	80	42	55	45	60	112	138	131	1092

Hilo (Hawaiʻi)

		Jan	Feb	Mar	Apr	May	June	July	Aug	Sept	Oct	Nov	Dec	Year
Max	T °F	79.8	79.2	79.5	79.8	81.2	82.7	83.0	83.6	83.8	83.2	84.4	80.0	81.5
	T °C	26.6	26.2	26.4	26.6	27.3	28.2	28.3	28.7	28.8	28.4	27.4	26.7	27.5
Min	T °F	63.6	63.6	64.4	65.5	66.5	67.6	68.6	68.9	68.6	68.1	66.8	64.8	66.4
	T °C	17.6	17.6	18.0	18.0	19.2	19.8	20.3	20.5	20.3	20.1	19.3	18.2	19.1

Hilo (Hawaiʻi)

		Jan	Feb	Mar	Apr	May	June	July	Aug	Sept	Oct	Nov	Dec	Year
Mn	T°F	71.7	71.7	72.0	72.7	73.9	75.2	75.8	76.3	76.2	75.7	74.2	72.4	74.0
	T°C	22.1	22.1	22.2	22.6	23.3	24.0	24.3	24.6	24.6	24.3	23.4	22.4	23.3
P	(in)	9.88	10.29	13.92	15.26	9.91	6.20	9.71	9.34	8.53	9.60	14.51	12.04	129.19
	(mm)	251	261	354	388	252	157	247	237	217	244	368	305	3281

Volcanoes National Park (Hawaiʻi)

		Jan	Feb	Mar	Apr	May	June	July	Aug	Sept	Oct	Nov	Dec	Year
Max	T°F	66.5	66.6	66.4	66.7	68.3	69.9	70.8	72.1	72.2	71.2	69.0	67.1	68.4
	T°C	19.2	19.2	19.1	19.3	20.2	21.1	21.6	22.3	22.4	21.8	20.6	19.5	20.2
Min	T°F	49.7	49.5	50.3	51.6	52.4	53.8	54.9	55.1	54.9	54.5	53.1	51.0	52.6
	T°C	9.8	9.7	10.2	10.9	11.3	12.1	12.7	12.8	12.7	12.5	11.7	10.6	11.4
Mn	T°F	58.3	58.1	58.4	59.2	60.4	61.8	62.9	63.7	63.6	62.9	61.1	59.1	60.8
	T°C	14.6	14.5	14.7	15.1	15.8	16.6	17.2	17.6	17.6	17.2	16.2	15.1	16.0
P	(in)	10.99	9.80	13.72	12.20	8.13	4.67	6.37	6.12	5.36	6.51	12.98	12.11	108.96
	(mm)	279	249	348	310	206	119	162	155	136	165	330	307	2766

Haleakalā Research Station (Maui)

		Jan	Feb	Mar	Apr	May	June	July	Aug	Sept	Oct	Nov	Dec	Year
Max	T°F	59.6	59.0	59.7	60.4	62.4	65.7	65.6	66.0	65.0	64.3	62.9	60.7	62.6
	T°C	15.3	15.0	15.4	15.8	16.9	18.7	18.7	18.9	18.3	17.9	17.2	15.9	17.0
Min	T°F	41.4	40.7	41.6	42.4	43.6	46.3	47.0	46.8	45.9	45.6	44.4	42.9	44.1
	T°C	5.2	4.8	5.3	5.8	6.4	7.9	8.3	8.2	7.7	7.6	6.9	6.1	6.7
Mn	T°F	50.5	49.9	50.7	51.4	52.0	56.1	56.3	56.5	55.5	55.0	53.9	51.8	52.4
	T°C	10.3	9.9	10.4	10.8	11.1	13.4	13.5	13.6	13.1	12.8	12.2	11.0	11.3
P	(in)	10.36	6.86	7.36	6.14	2.55	1.22	2.18	2.24	1.85	2.92	6.73	7.15	57.56
	(mm)	263	174	187	156	65	31	55	57	47	74	171	182	1462

Mauna Loa (Hawaiʻi)

		Jan	Feb	Mar	Apr	May	June	July	Aug	Sept	Oct	Nov	Dec	Year
Max	T°F	49.6	49.4	49.5	51.0	53.2	56.8	56.1	56.2	55.3	54.5	52.3	50.4	52.9
	T°C	9.8	9.7	9.7	10.6	11.8	13.8	13.4	13.4	12.9	12.5	11.3	10.2	11.6
Min	T°F	33.4	33.1	33.5	34.4	36.5	39.6	38.8	39.2	38.7	38.0	36.3	34.6	36.3
	T°C	0.8	0.6	0.8	1.3	2.5	4.2	3.8	4.0	3.7	3.3	2.4	1.4	2.4
Mn	T°F	41.5	41.2	41.8	42.7	44.9	48.2	47.8	47.8	47.0	46.2	44.3	42.5	44.6
	T°C	5.3	5.1	5.4	5.9	7.2	9.0	8.8	8.8	8.3	7.9	6.8	5.8	7.0
P	(in)	2.76	1.65	2.44	1.90	1.45	0.56	1.15	1.40	1.43	1.18	2.32	2.40	20.64
	(mm)	70	42	62	48	37	14	29	36	37	30	59	61	525

Haleakalā (Maui), and Hilo, Hawaii Volcanoes National Park, and Mauna Loa (Hawai'i). Temperature characteristics will be described here, and precipitation in Chapter 4. Note that August and September are the months of highest maximum temperature at sea level: Honolulu, 31.5°C (88.7°F), Lahaina, 31.4°C (88.6°F), and Hilo, 28.8°C (83.8°F). However, at the Hawaii Volcanoes National Park station, at 1,219 m (4,000 ft) elevation, summer maximum temperatures average only 22.4°C (72.3°F); at Haleakalā, at 2,144 m (7,100 ft), 18.9°C (66.0°F); and at Mauna Loa Observatory, at 3,400 m (11,200 ft), 13.4°C (56.2°F). Nighttime minimum temperatures, even during the hottest month, are a pleasant 23.3°C (74.0°F) for Honolulu and 20.5°C (68.9°F) for Hilo.

It is seen in Table 4 that the coolest months of the year at sea level in the Islands are January and February, with daytime highs at Honolulu and at Hilo averaging 26.2°C (79.2°F). Nighttime lows in winter are not very different from nighttime lows in summer, falling only to 18.6°C (65.4°F) in Honolulu and 17.6°C (63.6°F) in Hilo.

Graphs of the daily maximum and minimum temperatures for each month of the year for Honolulu, Haleakalā, and Mauna Loa are found in Figure 3.9. These graphs show the small range in temperature from winter to summer in Hawai'i: only 6°C (11°F) for maximum temperatures in Honolulu, less than 4°C (7°F) for Haleakalā, and 4.5°C (8°F) for Mauna Loa. Although the range throughout the year is similar at all elevations, the difference between daytime and nighttime temperatures in-

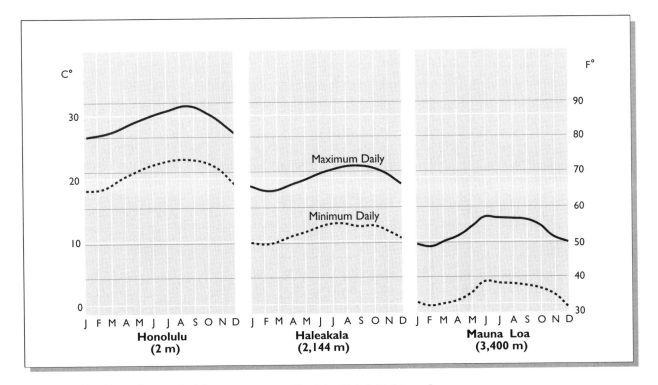

Figure 3.9 Monthly maximum and minimum temperatures: Honolulu, Haleakalā, Mauna Loa

creases with elevation because of clear skies above the inversion. At Mauna Loa, the daily range averages 9 °C (16 °F). It is important that climbers on the high mountains like Mauna Loa realize that nighttime temperatures could fall below freezing any month of the year.

The highest temperature ever measured in Hawai'i is 37.8 °C (100 °F), recorded at Pahala on the island of Hawai'i in April 1931, but temperatures above 35 °C (95 °F) are extremely rare. Apart from the dry leeward areas, temperatures of more than 32 °C (90 °F) are uncommon. These rare hot days occur when there are no winds blowing from the cooler ocean. The lowest temperature ever measured in Hawai'i is −12.8 °C (9 °F), recorded at the Mauna Kea Summit. However, at elevations below 305 m (1,000 ft), the lowest nighttime temperatures are in the 10–15 °C (50–59 °F) range. The lowest temperature ever recorded for Honolulu is 11 °C (52 °F).

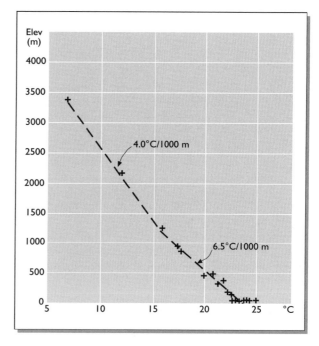

Figure 3.10 Average lapse rates in the Hawaiian Islands

Table 5 Mean Annual Temperatures (1961–1990) and Elevations Selected Hawaiian Stations

Station	Island	Temp. °C	Temp. °F	Elevation m	Elevation ft.
Haleakalā	Maui	11.3	52.4	2,144	7,100
Hawai'i Volcanoes National Park	Hawai'i	16.0	60.8	1,211	4,000
Hilo	Hawai'i	23.3	74.0	11	36
Honolulu Airport	O'ahu	25.1	77.2	2	6
Kahului	Maui	24.2	75.6	14	46
Kāne'ohe Mauka	O'ahu	23.6	74.5	69	228
Kohala Mission	Hawai'i	22.5	72.5	164	540
Lahaina	Maui	24.4	76.0	14	46
Līhu'e Airport	Kaua'i	24.2	75.6	31	102
Mānā	Kaua'i	23.9	75.0	3	10
Niu Ridge	O'ahu	22.1	71.7	381	1,260
'O'ōkala	Hawai'i	22.6	72.7	131	432
'Ōpae'ula	O'ahu	21.9	71.5	324	1,070
Mauna Loa	Hawai'i	7.0	44.6	3,400	11,200

Since there are few official temperature stations in Hawai'i, and probably also because of the relatively uniform temperatures at sea level, no maps of mean annual temperature have been published for the Islands. However, it is possible to draw such maps using the measured changes in temperature with elevation shown in Table 5 for selected stations, together with the topographic maps of the Islands, and we have attempted to do so using the following data.

The mean annual temperatures for the official stations shown in Table 5 are found to range from 7.0°C (44.6°F) for Mauna Loa to 25.1°C (77.2°F) for Honolulu. Plotting these mean annual tempera-

tures against elevation (Figure 3.10) makes it possible to estimate the average lapse rate (decline of temperature with elevation) for Hawai'i. It is observed that below approximately 1,200 m (3,900 ft), the lapse rate in Hawai'i is similar to the worldwide average of 6.5°C/1,000 m (3.6°F for 1,000 ft). However, above 1,200 m (3,900 ft), the approximate height of the trade wind inversion, the lapse rate is smaller—about 4°C/1,000 m (3°F for 1,000 ft).

It is possible then, by plotting the data from Table 4 onto contour maps of the Islands, and using the appropriate lapse rates, to construct maps of mean annual temperature for the Islands (Figure 3.11).

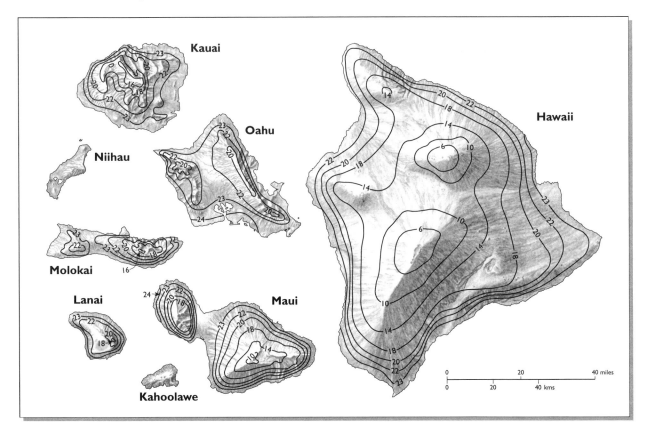

Figure 3.11 Average annual temperatures (°C) in the Islands

Most of the coastal stations have annual temperatures of 23–24 °C (73–75 °F), with the highest annual temperatures in West Maui along the Lahaina coast, and on the south coast of Oʻahu. The summit of Haleakalā has a mean annual temperature of only 10 °C (50 °F), similar to that of Detroit, Michigan, while the summits of Mauna Kea and Mauna Loa have average annual temperatures of less than 6 °C (43 °F), similar to those in southern Alaska. On Maui and the Big Island, the large range in temperatures is soon discovered by visitors to the high elevations.

SUGGESTED READINGS

Blumenstock and Price. 1967. (See complete citation in list of references).

Charnell, R. L. 1967. Long-wave radiation near the Hawaiian Islands. *Journal Geophysical Research* 72 (2): 489–495.

Ekern, P. C. 1965b. The fraction of sunlight retained as net radiation in Hawaii. *Journal Geophysical Research* 70 (4): 785–793.

Ekern, P. C. 1978. Variation in sunlight induced by topography under the trade wind regime on Oahu, Hawaii. *Proceedings: Conference on Climate and Energy.* Asheville, North Carolina: American Meteorological Society.

How, K. T. S. 1978. *Solar radiation in Hawaii: 1933–1975.* Honolulu: Department of Land and Natural Resources (Report R57).

Mendonca, B. G.; Hanson, K. J.; and Deluisi, J. J. 1978. Volcanically related secular trends in atmospheric transmission at Mauna Loa Observatory, Hawaii. *Science* 202:513–515.

Nullet, D. 1987. Energy sources for evaporation on tropical islands. *Physical Geography* 8 (1): 36–45.

Nullet, D., and Giambelluca, T. W. 1992. Radiation climatology through the trade-wind inversion. *Physical Geography* 13 (1): 66–80.

Yoshihara, T., and Ekern, P. C. 1978. *Assessment of the potential of solar energy in Hawaii.* Honolulu: The Hawaii Natural Energy Institute, University of Hawaii.

CHAPTER 4

The Water Balance and Climatic Classification

Tom Giambelluca and Marie Sanderson

Introduction

Water is a crucially important element in our natural environment and is essential to all forms of life. Many features of the earth's surface are a result of the movement of water—in rivers and glaciers, for example—and the climates of the earth are profoundly affected by the distribution and movement of water.

Water use includes direct consumption, irrigation of crops, industrial processing, transportation, and recreation. All of these depend on the availability of water. Whether or not water is available depends on the movement of water between ocean and atmosphere, atmosphere and land, and land and ocean—the "hydrologic cycle." Water often changes from one to another of its three states of gas, liquid, and solid through evaporation, condensation, freezing, and melting. All are important parts of the hydrologic cycle. Since these processes use or release energy, the cycling of water is connected with the cycling of energy in the environment that we discussed in Chapter 3.

Flows of water within the hydrologic cycle are measured or estimated using the concept of water balance. In practice, the water balance is usually applied to a part of the hydrologic cycle called "the soil-plant system," which includes an area of the earth's surface, the plants growing on it, and the soil penetrated by the plants' roots. The water balance is a simple accounting system that monitors inflows and outflows and changes in the amount of water stored in the soil-plant system. The principal inflow of water to the system is precipitation, although in some parts of the world, agricultural irrigation or urban lawn sprinkling are also important inflows. Outflows are evaporation, transpiration by plants, surface and subsurface runoff, and downward drainage of water that recharges underlying groundwater. The characteristics of the soil, the density and kind of vegetation, the depth of root penetration, and the amount of water stored in the soil play important roles in governing the outflow processes. A simple equation illustrates the water balance concept:

$$P + I = R + E + Q + S$$

where P = precipitation, I = irrigation, R = runoff, E = evapotranspiration, Q = groundwater recharge, and S = change in soil moisture storage.

In Hawai'i, the climate, soil, and vegetation, which determine the water balance, have large gradients. Most of the perceived differences among the environments of Hawai'i can be attributed to differences in the water balance. Because the water balance integrates the influences of solar radiation, the state of the atmosphere, and the surface characteristics of a region, it is sometimes used to classify climates, as will be seen later in the chapter.

The water balance has also been used for many practical purposes in Hawai'i. Rainfall which percolates into the soil and drains beyond the plant-root zone recharges the aquifers on the Islands. Pesticide contamination can occur when drainage water carries the chemicals beneath the surface. On O'ahu, where municipal water supplies are derived mainly from groundwater, the water balance method has been used to assess the amount of water that can safety be withdrawn from wells and to study problems of groundwater contamination by pesticides (see Chapter 5). Throughout the state, the timing of irrigation for sugarcane and other crops is decided by estimating soil moisture using the water balance method.

Figure 4.1 shows the principal water flows and storage components of the hydrologic cycle in Hawai'i. Rainfall is the major water source. Some

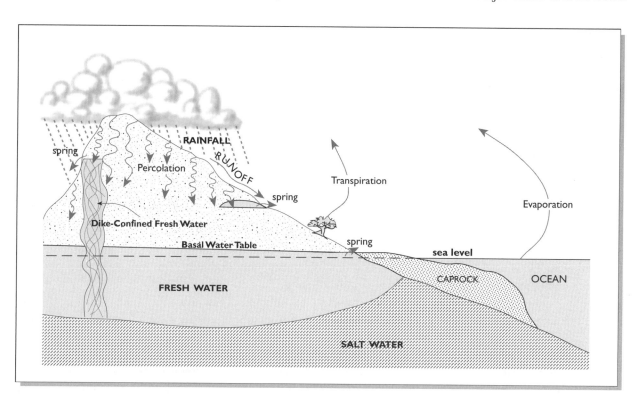

Figure 4.1 Hydrologic cycle in Hawai'i

rainwater may flow over the land surface as runoff, some evaporates or transpires from plants, and the rest is stored in the soil or percolates downward to recharge the groundwater. Groundwater is an important feature of the hydrology of the Islands. Fresh water percolating through the porous soils and rocks of the Islands' interiors moves downward until a less-porous layer is encountered, or until salt water is reached. There, the fresh water may accumulate in the porous rock (aquifer) and saturate the lower portion. Fresh water also accumulates in aquifers confined by impervious rock walls, called "dikes." The upper surface of the saturated zone is called a water table. If the water table is inclined, water within the saturated zone will flow down the water table gradient, eventually emerging as a spring. These can be on land or beneath the ocean surface near shore.

Most groundwater is found just above the salt water that penetrates the Islands' interiors from the surrounding ocean. This basal groundwater forms a lens-shaped body called a Ghyben-Herzberg lens. The lighter fresh water floats on the underlying salt water, depressing it downward about 40 m for every 1 m (40 ft for 1 ft) that the freshwater rises above sea level. Even though the basal water table is only a few meters above sea level, a huge volume of fresh water is stored beaneath it. The basal lens is maintained by a constant inflow of infiltrating water. Water in the lens flows toward the coast, discharging in springs along the shoreline and along the ocean floor near the coast. A formation of less permeable sediments and ancient corals found along some coasts acts as a "caprock," inhibiting freshwater flow toward the ocean and allowing a higher water table to be attained.

In this chapter, each element of the water balance of the Hawaiian Islands will be described: rainfall, runoff, evapotranspiration (the sum of evaporation and transpiration), and ground water recharge.

Rainfall

Of the climatic elements, rainfall is probably the most easily measured, and for this reason there are more and longer records of rainfall than of temperature, wind, humidity, solar radiation, or any other climatic feature. It may also be argued that rainfall is the most important climatic element, having the greatest effect on humanity and the physical and biological environment. This is certainly true in the tropics, where spatial and temporal variability of temperature is small and distinctions among various climates result primarily from differences in the amount, frequency, intensity, seasonality, and variability of rainfall.

Prior to 1976, a total of 1,985 rain gage sites were operated at one time or another in Hawai'i for various periods of time. Several factors have contributed to the large number of gages. Plantation agriculture (sugarcane and pineapple) dominated the economy of Hawai'i for much of this century. The growers developed and practiced advanced methods of maximizing crop yields that required detailed environmental data, especially water availability. The joint Pineapple Research Institute–Hawaiian Sugar Planters Association and the University of Hawaii's Meteorology Department established a dense network of gages, and collected, collated, and published data. In addition, water purveyors like the Honolulu Board of Water Supply, and other agencies including the National Weather Service and the U.S. Geological Survey, as well as many private citizens, maintained rain gages throughout the state.

The topic of Hawaiian rainfall has long fascinated scientists and laypeople for a variety of meteorological, hydrological, and agricultural reasons. One of the first extended monographs published by the American Meteorological Society was devoted to Hawaiian rainfall. Project Shower and the Warm Rain Project, comprehensive studies of orographic cloud dynamics and rainfall on the island of Hawai'i, are important landmarks in the understanding of the mechanics of warm rainfall. The many other published reports, too numerous for a complete listing here, range from analysis of rainfall-runoff relationships to empirical orthogonal function analysis.

Rainfall observations in Hawai'i date from the 1840s. Over the years, numerous maps of Hawaiian rainfall have been prepared. The most comprehensive effort was that of Taliaferro (1959), who prepared monthly and annual median rainfall maps for all the major islands, based on a common twenty-five-year base period (1933–1957). These maps were the standard for nearly three decades. More recently, Meisner undertook the task of updating and revising Taliaferro's maps. He sought out and compiled all existing rainfall data and developed a methodology for adjusting normals to a common base period (sixty years for most islands). That work led to a revised set of median annual maps for the state by Meisner, Schroeder, and Ramage, and eventually to a complete set of monthly and annual maps showing median and mean rainfall, published in 1986.

Rainfall Measurement

Rainfall is measured today in much the same manner as it was for the first recorded measurements six centuries ago in Korea, using some type of receptacle with a horizontally oriented orifice.

Recording gages make a continuous record of rainfall, allowing determination of short-duration intensities. Studies of rainfall frequency and real-time rainfall monitoring for flood warning rely on recording gage data. Nonrecording gages consist of a receptacle in which water is read at regular or irregular intervals. The National Weather Service maintains a network of nonrecording and recording gages in Hawai'i. Monthly precipitation averages (1961–1990) for seven stations are given in Table 4. In remote, high-rainfall areas, regular readings are impractical, so large-capacity storage gages are used. Nonstandard gages, such as plastic cylinders or wedges designed for easy mounting and reading, are also used. Private citizens who have installed such gages and maintain records provide valuable information in areas lacking standard gages.

Despite the apparent ease of rain collection, interpretation is fraught with uncertainty, particularly using a single point value to represent a large area. Even in Hawai'i, with its high average gage density (0.125 gage/km² [0.325 gage/mi²]), the entire rain-gage network comprises a very small sample of the area which it represents (less than 1:250 million). Because rainfall is generally perceived to have some degree of spatial continuity, a well-situated gage is expected to give a good indication of the rainfall received in the surrounding area. But when adjacent gages often give significantly different results, we must question how representative any one rainfall measurement can be. Rain gages in Hawai'i are clustered mainly in agricultural and urban areas, with very few in the wetter mountainous areas. This uneven coverage adds uncertainty to estimates of water availability on the Islands.

In addition to errors arising from the small sample size, measurement itself is subject to error. Rain-catch efficiency is most notably affected by wind, because the gage interferes with the air stream moving past it, and flow over the orifice tends to accelerate and become turbulent above the gage. This acceleration and turbulence reduce the rain catch. Thus wind is a major source of error in nearly all rainfall measurements. A gage exposed to a 4.4 m/s (10 mph) wind catches only 90% as much rain as a gage in calm conditions. Higher winds reduce the rain catch still more.

Median Annual Rainfall Maps

Probably the most frequently used statistics of any data set are those that describe the central tendency of the distribution, the most familiar of which are the median and the mean. The selection of the appropriate statistic for rainfall often depends on the application. For many purposes, the median, defined as the value for which higher or lower occurrences are equally frequent, is preferred as an indicator of average rainfall.

Because the Hawaiian rainfall data include stations with various record lengths, a special statistical technique was applied to adjust for such differences when computing the median. Annual median rainfall maps of the islands of Hawai'i, Maui, Moloka'i, Lāna'i, O'ahu, and Kaua'i (developed from adjusted values) are shown in Figure 4.2.

The spatial gradient of open-ocean rainfall over an area as small as that occupied by the Hawaiian Islands would be nearly imperceptible. Estimates of annual average open-ocean rainfall near Hawai'i currently range from approximately 560 mm (22 in) to 700 mm (28 in), yet on the Islands themselves, average annual rainfall ranges from less than 250 mm (10 in) to more than 11,000 mm (430 in). Obviously the Islands themselves are responsible for these variations. Clouds and rainfall develop when

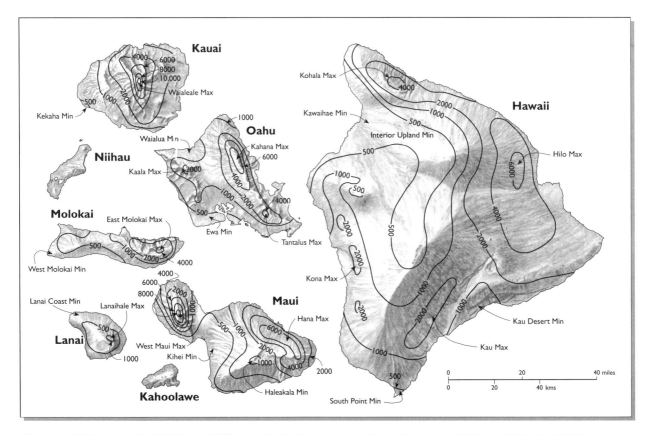

Figure 4.2 Median annual rainfall (mm) (Ni'ihau and Kaho'olawe, no data) (from Giambelluca, Nullet, and Schroeder 1986)

air is cooled, usually as a result of its ascent. The primary rainfall-producing mechanism in Hawai'i is orographic lifting of moisture-laden northeast trade winds over the windward slopes of each island, as was explained in Chapter 2. In addition, thermally driven diurnal circulations (sea breeze–land breeze systems and mountain–valley winds) contribute to rainfall by reinforcing trade wind–orographic lifting, by inducing areas of low-level convergence with the prevailing trades, or by producing orographic uplift in areas not exposed to trades. Convective uplift occurs on the larger islands, often in conjunction with the sea-breeze circulation. Open-ocean rainfall near Hawai'i is almost exclusively produced by large-scale storm systems. Drier areas of the state receive most of their rainfall from such storms.

In general, Hawaiian rainfall is greatest in regions of persistent uplifting, and least in leeward areas and atop the highest mountains. On the lee side of mountains, the air subsides as a warm dry wind after being heated by condensation and dessicated by precipitation fallout during its ascent over the orographic barrier. Dry, high mountain areas lie above the inversion that prevents further upslope flow of moist air.

The rainfall patterns shown in Figure 4.2 are worth describing in more detail. On the island of Hawai'i, four areas of rainfall maxima are found: Kohala, in the windward Kohala Mountains; Hilo, on the eastern slopes of Mauna Kea; Ka'ū, on Mauna Loa's southeastern flank; and upslope from the Kona Coast. Four areas of minimum rainfall also occur: at Kawaihae on the South Kohala Coast; in the interior uplands at high elevations in the central part of the island; in the Ka'ū Desert, leeward of Kīlauea Volcano; and at South Point, the southern tip of the island.

The Kohala and Hilo maxima are examples of orographic rainfall associated with sea breeze-aided trade winds. The Kohala Mountains maximum occurs on the windward side near their 1,670 m (5,480 ft) peak. Rainfall decreases steeply on the Kohala Mountains' leeward side, toward the Kawaihae minimum. The Hilo maximum, found on the broad eastern slopes of Mauna Kea at about 760 m (2,500 ft), clearly shows the influence of the trade wind inversion. The presence of the inversion at about 2,000 m (6,560 ft), as well as the configuration of the island with its high mountains, together tend to split the circulation and divert upslope flow around, rather than over, the higher elevations. Trade wind rainfall maxima on the Islands' lower mountains generally occur at or near their summits. As a result of the cap on upslope flow and its being diverted by the inversion, rainfall maxima on mountains higher than 2,000 m (6,560 ft), such as Mauna Kea, are found at lower elevations.

The Ka'ū maximum is unique in Hawai'i because it occurs along a southeast-oriented slope. A diurnal rainfall maximum occurs in the afternoon, characteristic of a thermal forcing, but wind direction indicates that orographic lift does occur as air moves over Kīlauea and passes over the south flank of Mauna Loa. Satellite imagery shows cloud is present at sunrise as would be expected where orographic lifting is occurring. The normal trade wind direction (approximately N 70°E) results in an upslope trajectory. Orographic lifting is enhanced by a thermally induced circulation up the heated slopes during the day, and intense rainfall occurs here with southeasterly winds during winter storms.

The Kona rainfall maximum, extending along a strip at about 600 to 900 m (2,000 to 3,000 ft) elevation, is also unique. While the sea-breeze flow has a slight effect on rainfall in other leeward areas of the state, the effect is most pronounced in Kona. Trade wind sheltering by Mauna Loa and Hualālai and afternoon heating of the west-facing slopes provide conditions for a well-developed sea breeze during the day. The trade wind flow around the island swirls in from the west and thus enhances the sea breeze. This stream then converges with trade winds that may sneak over the saddle between Mauna Loa and Mauna Kea.

The effects of the Kohala Mountains and Mauna Kea make Kawaihae the driest area in the state. Dry, subsiding air funneled through the saddle between the two mountain masses prevails here. The interior uplands minimum includes most of the area above the trade wind inversion. Kīlauea has its own rain shadow. The annual rainfall decreases by 1,250 mm (50 in)/yr between the Hawaii Volcanoes National Park Headquarters on the northeast rim of the Caldera and Halemaʻumaʻu parking lot 5 km to the southwest. The leeward slope of Kīlauea is called the Kaʻū Desert. The rains are less frequent, but the porosity of the lavas adds to the desert effect since the rain disappears underground. The South Point minimum is associated with its position in the lee of Mauna Loa. Also involved is the speed divergence that results when the trade winds cross the coast and escape the retarding influence of friction with the land surface.

On Maui, the rainfall pattern is strongly affected by the two volcanic peaks of Haleakalā and Puʻu Kukui. The two rainfall maxima are near Hāna, on the northeastern slope of Haleakalā, and at Puʻu Kukui, the summit of the West Maui mountains. As with the Hilo maximum, the Hāna maximum occurs at approximately 650 m (2,130 ft) elevation. Here too, upslope flow is capped by the inversion. Puʻu Kukui is cone-shaped, and orographic rainfall at the summit can occur with wind from any direction. The deeply incised valleys enhance uplift by funnelling air toward the summit. As a result, West Maui rainfall exceeds 9,000 mm (350 in) annually, the second highest in Hawaiʻi.

At Kīhei, on the west coast of East Maui, the rainfall minimum stems from strong divergence of the trade winds after they pass between the two

mountains. The leeward coast of West Maui, from Mākena to Kāʻanapali, is also dry. The Haleakalā secondary minimum, like the interior uplands minimum on Hawaiʻi, lies above the trade wind inversion.

The rainfall pattern of Molokaʻi closely resembles the island's topography. The East Molokaʻi rainfall maximum occurs near the East Molokaʻi mountain summit, while the West Molokaʻi minimum includes most of the coastal portion of western Molokaʻi. The orographic uplifting of the trade winds is responsible for the East Molokaʻi maximum. Despite its substantial height, East Molokaʻi has a lower rainfall maximum than other peaks in Hawaiʻi, presumably because the mountain's ridgeline is oriented nearly parallel to the trades. The east-west elongation of the secondary rainfall maximum across West Molokaʻi may result from the orographic cloud plume described earlier.

The small area and subdued topography of Lānaʻi produce a single rainfall maximum, at Lānaʻihale near the island's highest point. The island's position in the lee of East Molokaʻi and West Maui keeps this island relatively dry.

Oʻahu, with two roughly parallel mountain ranges oriented nearly perpendicular to the northeast trade winds, has three rainfall maxima: at Kahana, just to the lee and northwest of the center of the Koʻolau ridgeline; Tantalus, leeward of the highest point in the Koʻolau Range, and Kaʻala, at the highest point of the Waiʻanae Range. Areas of minimum rainfall occur at Waialua, on the coast north of the island's saddle area, and in the ʻEwa area, along the southwest shores of Oʻahu.

The Kahana and Tantalus maxima are the result of strong uplifting of the trade winds along the steep windward Koʻolau slope. The tendency for the maximum rainfall to occur leeward of the crest line has been attributed to the continued upward motion and subsequent rapid downturning of the air stream after cresting the ridge as well as to wind-blown rain. The trade winds, partially dessicated after crossing the Koʻolau Range, produce relatively less rain when lifted over the Waiʻanae Range. The Waialua and ʻEwa minima are found in the lee of the Koʻolau Range.

Rainfall on Kauaʻi is characterized by a single maximum at Waiʻaleʻale, near the island's highest point, Kawaikini. With an annual median rainfall of 11,278 mm (444 in), it is the wettest location in the state. Cherapungi in Assam in the foothills of the Himalayas is Waiʻaleʻale's principal rival as the world's wettest spot. A mere 25 km (15 mi) southwest of Waiʻaleʻale, and in its shadow, the Kekaha coastal areas receive less than 500 mm (20 in) of rain a year.

Rainfall Seasons

The seasonal distribution of rainfall differs from place to place in Hawaiʻi, but certain features are common to areas with similar exposures. As we saw in Chapter 1, the ancient Hawaiians recognized two seasons: *kau* (May–October), the high-sun period corresponding to warmth and steady trade winds; and *hoʻoilo* (November–April), the cooler period when trade winds are less frequent, and widespread storm rainfall is more common. Climatologists today agree with the two-season concept, although a five-month "summer" (May–September) and seven-month "winter" (October–April) are generally used.

The winter-wet, summer-dry rainfall regime is familiar to most Hawaiʻi residents. For much of the state, the wettest month is January and the driest June (see Table 4). This is particularly true for dry, leeward areas. Wet areas, however, have less annual variation. For instance, at ʻEke, near the West Maui high-rainfall area, the wettest month (November) has about twice as much rain as the driest month (June). By contrast, at Maui's leeward coastal station at Lahaina, the ratio is 50:1. Wet areas are usu-

ally characterized by three maxima and three minima. Peaks in the annual cycle are observed in March or April, August, and November or December, and lows are found in February, June, and September or October.

Winter rainfall maxima in dry areas arise from the greater frequency of synoptic storm systems in that season. In the wet areas, orographic rainfall increases in summer as a result of the more constant trade winds. Wet, mountainous areas also receive heavy rainfall from winter storms. But because trade winds are less frequent in winter, these areas do not exhibit the strong winter-maximum rainfall cycle characteristic of drier parts of the Islands.

In Kona, on the Big Island's west coast, the chief rainfall-producing mechanism is the convergence of the sea breeze with trade winds. The summer season is thus the wettest, since this is the season in which the trades are more frequent. On the island of Hawaiʻi, February is relatively dry. Of course, February is two or three days shorter than the other months. In addition, however, the atmospheric trough which is located west of the Islands during most of the winter usually shifts east of the Islands during February, producing a slight decline in rainfall.

Intense Rainfall

For many practical purposes, the probability of brief periods of intense rainfall is more important than annual or monthly averages. Surface runoff produced by high-intensity rain can lead to flooding and soil erosion. Site selection and design of bridges, drainage systems, and flood control devices, evaluation of flood hazard, and planning for soil conservation require information on the probability of intense rainfall. Such information is derived from rain gage records and presented in the form of graphs relating rainfall amount for a particular duration (such as one hour or twenty-four hours) to probability of occurrence, usually expressed in terms of a return period. The return period gives the average number of years between occurrences of rainfall of given amounts. By assessing rainfall probability at many stations, it is possible to map the spatial distribution of intense rainfall.

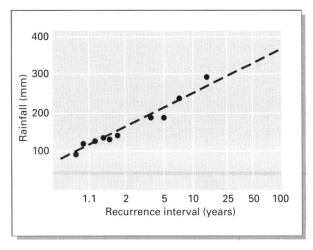

Figure 4.3 24-hour maximum rainfall versus return period at Mt. Ka'ala on O'ahu (from Giambelluca et al. 1984)

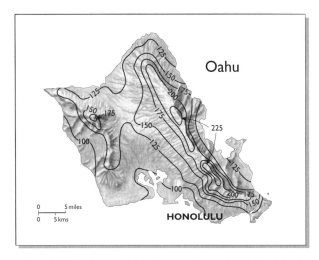

Figure 4.4 The pattern of 24-hour maximum rainfall (mm) for the two-year return period on O'ahu (from Giambelluca et al. 1984)

A graph of twenty-four-hour maximum rainfall versus return period at Ka'ala on O'ahu is shown in Figure 4.3. The graph is plotted on specially-scaled axes that allow the relationship to be depicted by a straight line. The spatial pattern of intense rainfall on O'ahu is illustrated in Figure 4.4, which shows the amount of twenty-four-hour rainfall which would be equaled or exceeded, on average, once every two years. Note that the pattern resembles that of median annual rainfall on the island, with the highest values found near the crest of the Ko'olau Range, and the lowest values along the leeward coast.

Fog Drip

A mass of clouds clinging to the steep mountain slopes is a familar sight in Hawai'i. The trade winds, forced to ascend the mountains, produce the persistent mountain-hugging clouds. As the cloud droplets move over the barrier, many come into contact with the leaves and branches of the forest. Thus, cloud droplets are scavenged from the wind, wetting the vegetation, and eventually dripping down to moisten the soil. Interception of cloud droplets by vegetation contributes significant quantities of moisture to the soil in cloud-shrouded areas. Field measurements have been made on various mountain slopes in Hawai'i to estimate the amount of water intercepted from the clouds. In an area of West Maui, evidence was found that fog drip contributes a significant amount of moisture to elevated land surfaces. Along the leeward slopes of the Ko'olau Range on O'ahu, the area above the cloud base at approximately 610 m (2,000 ft) receives about 230 mm (9 in) of fog drip annually. In such areas, the natural vegetation is able to survive, despite low rainfall, because of moisture provided in this way.

Methods of augmenting the precipitation on Lāna'i have included efforts at capturing this fog drip. Ridges on Lāna'i have been planted with

Norfolk Island Pines that can be seen while driving around the northern edge of Lānaʻihale toward the windward coast. Other efforts have involved constructing wire traps to capture the cloud water. In parts of the world with little rainfall but frequent fog, harvesting of fog drip can provide a valuable water source where other alternatives are lacking.

Runoff

In the wet areas of Hawaiʻi, numerous small streams carry runoff toward the ocean. Generally, a high percentage of rainfall becomes runoff during intense or prolonged rainstorms. The type of soil and land use also affects the amount of runoff. Impervious roofs and streets greatly increase runoff from urban areas. Cultivation generally compacts the soil, resulting in more runoff. Fresh lava flows, on the other hand, are so permeable that no runoff is observed.

Because of the geology and steep terrain of the Hawaiian Islands, streams rise and fall quickly in response to heavy rain, while between storms, flow may cease. These characteristics limit the use of surface water in some areas of Hawaiʻi. The surface water resources of the state consist mainly of small reservoirs and the diversion of streams directly into irrigation systems. Streams support natural habitats for many of the endemic plants and animals of Hawaiʻi, and they provide recreational, aesthetic, and cultural benefits. Thousands of waterfalls flow intermittently, providing spectacular scenery. The same streams and waterfalls acting over thousands of years have shaped the Islands, sculpting valleys and building coastal plains. But runoff can also be an agent of destruction; flash floods arrive with little warning and with devastating force.

Runoff can be estimated by measuring streamflow or by using a formula relating runoff to rainfall. Such measurements and estimates for southern

Oʻahu were used to derive an equation relating annual runoff to annual rainfall. Figure 4.5 shows the distribution of average annual runoff for Hawaiʻi as estimated by this equation. The small scale of these maps does not permit the effects of land use, soil type, and other surface characteristics to be depicted; these effects are discussed in Chapter 5.

Evapotranspiration

In nature, water enters the earth's atmosphere through evaporation at the earth's surface. This change of state from liquid water to water vapor can occur at any exposed, moist surface. Evaporation from the tissue of living plants is called transpiration, and it is usually the dominant form of evaporation from vegetated surfaces such as forest or cropland. Water is absorbed from the soil by plant roots and transported to the leaves, where it evaporates from the moist inner surfaces of minute cavities called stomata. The flow of water from roots to leaves that is induced by transpiration serves like a bloodstream to carry nutrients. Because transpiration is also a cooling process, it helps prevent damage to the plant from midday heat. The term evapotranspiration (ET), evaporation plus transpiration, is often used to describe all water loss from the surface of the earth into the atmosphere.

Energy for ET is derived from net radiation and advection (as explained in Chapter 3). Movement of water vapor away from the surface is dependent on the amount of turbulent airflow and the dryness of the air. In general, higher wind speeds and rougher surfaces increase turbulence and result in greater ET. To estimate ET, it is convenient to use the concept of potential evapotranspiration (PE), defined as the ET rate observed when water is readily available to a vegetated surface. PE depends on many factors: solar radiation, air temperature, wind speed, relative humidity, and surface characteristics. PE can be

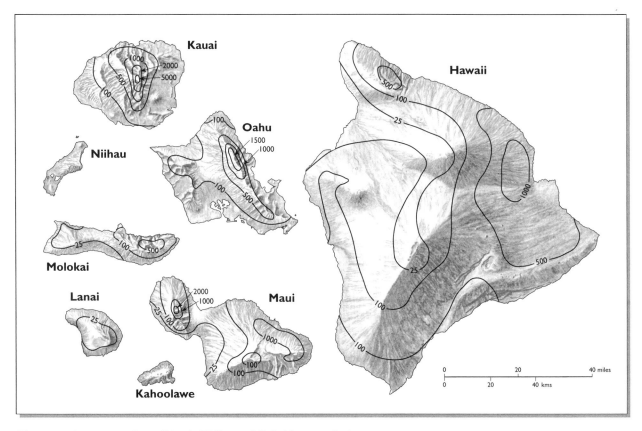

Figure 4.5 Average annual runoff (mm) (Niʻihau and Kahoʻolawe, no data)

measured directly with the use of a specialized instrument called a lysimeter, but, because of the expense and difficulty of operating a lysimeter, PE is usually estimated by other means. For example, PE is commonly based on measurements of open-water evaporation from pans. In addition, in climatic literature, there are various formulae for estimating PE on the basis of meteorological measurements.

Data from evaporation pans have been widely used in Hawaiʻi for estimating PE from sugarcane and pineapple fields. In rainy areas, pan data have been supplemented with evaporation measurements from small, specially developed porous surface atmometers. Figure 4.6 features maps of average

annual pan evaporation. The relationship between evaporation and net radiation can be seen by comparing this figure with the map of net radiation (Figure 3.7). Highest pan evaporation rates are found in the sunny, hot leeward areas, while the lowest values occur in the cloudy areas along the windward mountain slopes. Evaporation rates on the upper slopes of the high mountains on Maui and Hawaiʻi, above the inversion, are increased by the intense radiation and low humidity.

Potential evapotranspiration represents the atmospheric demand for water vapor. The actual evapotranspiration that occurs depends also on the availability of water. For a very moist surface, or over

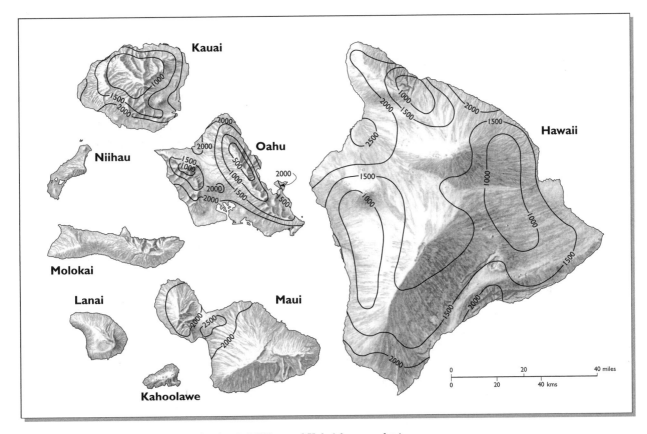

Figure 4.6 Average annual pan evaporation (mm) (Niʻihau and Kahoʻolawe, no data)

open water, ET will equal PE. But a completely dry surface will yield no moisture to the atmosphere regardless of the amount of energy, wind speed, or the humidity and temperature of the air. Over a vegetated surface, ET may eventually remove enough water from the soil that plants can no longer extract water fast enough to meet the demand. Then ET decreases below PE. To estimate the loss of water, it is necessary to determine PE and to estimate the amount of available soil moisture by means of a water balance accounting procedure.

Besides soil type, the depth and density of plant roots influence the availability of soil moisture. Root development varies according to species, age, and health of the vegetation. Physiological differences among plant species also affect the amount of water they use. A comparison of the Islands' two major plantation crops, sugarcane and pineapple, illustrates the effects of plant factors on ET. Sugarcane transpires water freely. As the crop matures, the ET of a sugarcane field increases and may eventually equal or exceed the pan evaporation rate. Pineapple, on the other hand, is a water-conserving plant. Its thick, waxy leaves, and stomata that close during the day limit pineapple transpiration to about 20% of the pan evaporation rate. As the crop matures, the ET of a pineapple field declines. The water-conserving properties of a pineapple crop cause substantial changes in the regional water balance. Because ET is lowered in a pineapple field, groundwater recharge is increased. The effects of pineapple and other crops on the water balance will be discussed in Chapter 5.

Groundwater Recharge

As water infiltrates the soil, some adheres to the soil particles and remains in the root zone available for ET. Soil texture and root depth largely determine how much water can be held in storage. If more water enters the soil than the soil can hold, the excess water percolates beyond the roots and eventually makes its way to the water table, recharging the groundwater. The groundwater flowing from springs or being pumped from wells, shafts, and tunnels originates in this way. This recharge depends mainly on rainfall. The irrigation of agricultural crops can be a major contributor to groundwater recharge, as well as the sprinkling of lawns and gardens in urban areas. The amount of runoff and the rate of ET also affect the recharge rate.

In Hawai'i, groundwater provides most of the water used in agriculture, industry, and in the municipal water supply systems. The amount of groundwater recharge can be estimated using the water balance technique. In one such study on O'ahu, annual recharge was related to annual rainfall, and maps of the average annual recharge rates in the state were derived (Figure 4.7). The calcula-

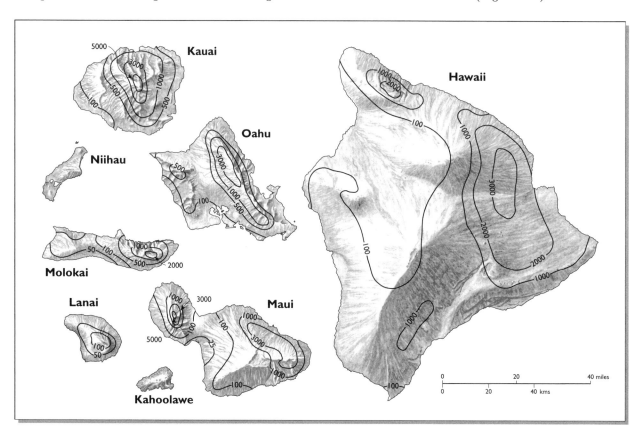

Figure 4.7 Average annual groundwater recharge (mm) (Ni'ihau and Kaho'olawe, no data)

tions are representative of a natural land surface and do not show the effects of agriculture and urbanization, which have important impacts on the recharge, as will be seen in the next chapter.

Using the Water Balance to Classify Hawaiian Climate

Like most other environmental variables, climate can be classified, but the task is more difficult than, for example, vegetation or soils classification. Classifying climates is important, however, since it permits the identification of similar climate types on a worldwide basis, and the drawing of climatic maps.

We owe the first classification of climate to the Greek philosopher Aristotle, whose system was used until the scientific measurement of climatic parameters began in the nineteenth century. The early attempts to classify climates were made by biologists, who were interested in the climatic reasons for the distribution of various types of vegetation. World classifications of climate of necessity had to await world maps of climatic elements, such as temperature and precipitation. The first maps of mean monthly world temperatures were published by the German climatologist Dove in 1848.

In the latter years of the nineteenth century, Koeppen, a German biologist, published the first quantitative classification of world climates, using Dove's maps. Koeppen's classification used plants as climatic indicators, and was based primarily on temperature. He designated his climates A, B, C, D, and E, with A the hottest (torrid zone) climates, and E the coldest (frigid zone) climates. Koeppen's climatic boundaries were chosen to correspond to vegetation boundaries. For example, the poleward boundary of the A climates, represented by the 18 °C (64.4 °F) annual isotherm, marked the limit of the tropical rain forest. A second letter in the classification indicated the moisture regime (e.g., s = summer dry and w = winter dry).

Although criticized for its empirical approach and minor attention to the moisture factor in climate, the Koeppen classification is still widely used today, since it can be applied to any station with monthly temperature and precipitation data. We show in Figure 4.8 the climates of the island of Hawai'i according to this classification (from Juvik et al. 1978). The classification uses monthly mean temperatures for fifty-five island stations, either measured or extrapolated using elevation–temperature relationships.

The four broad Koeppen climatic zones on the island of Hawai'i are organized primarily as concentric altitudinal bands on the mountain slopes. Humid, tropical A climates occupy the lower slopes from sea level to about 450 m (1,350 ft), and slightly higher in warmer areas of leeward Kona. The Koeppen system distinguishes two subtypes in the B climate classification on the basis of relative aridity: the true desert, BW (the W referring to the German word *wüste*, meaning wasteland) and the semidesert BS (steppe) climate. A small area of desert BW climate appears on the west coast, centered on Kawaihae. Inland, where it rains 190 mm (7.5 in) a year leeward of the Kohala Mountains, the true desert gives way to a semidesert BS climate that extends southward to Kailua.

In the Koeppen classification, C climates require the temperature of the coldest month to be between –3° and 18 °C (28° and 64 °F). Thus, as a result of the moderating influence of altitude, almost two-thirds of the "tropical" island of Hawai'i possesses a temperate climate.

An E climate signifies that the temperature of the warmest month is below 10 °C (50 °F). Trees will not normally grow where mean temperatures fall below this level. Hence, E climates characterize the treeless arctic tundra. Above the 3,200 m (10,500 ft) level on the high mountains in Hawai'i, all months have a mean temperature below 10 °C (50 °F), so these climates on the Big Island are classified E.

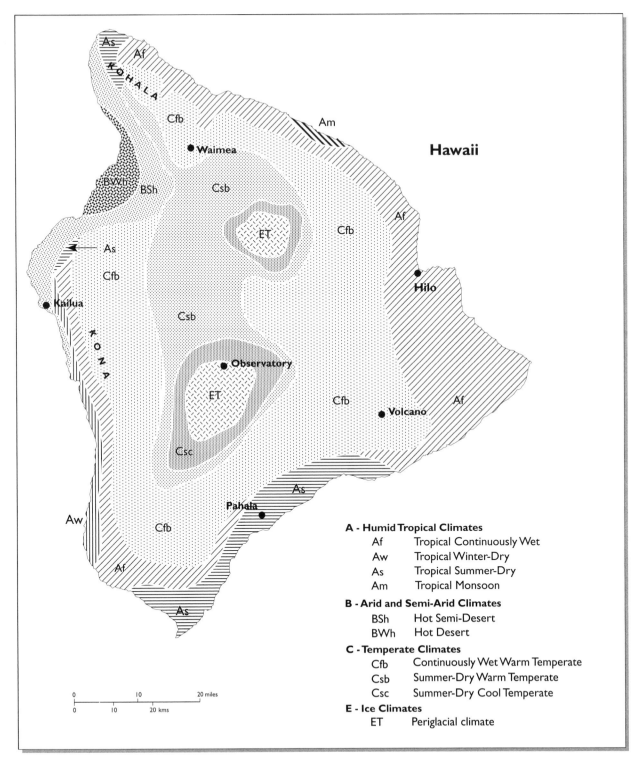

Figure 4.8 Distribution of Koeppen climate types on the island of Hawai'i (after Juvik et al., 1978)

The preceding discussion of the Koeppen climatic zones on Hawai'i says little about the direct linkage of climate to physical and biological processes at the earth/atmosphere interface. What is required in a climatic classification is an integration of seasonal moisture supply (or rainfall) with the evaporation and transpiration demands (or potential evapotranspiration) of the vegetation that would provide an index of moisture surplus or deficit. This would lead to an understanding of the relationships between climate and the terrestrial ecosystems. In 1948, the American climatologist Thornthwaite based his climate classification on this relationship of water need, or potential evapotranspiration, to water supply, or precipitation.

Thornthwaite's classification is based on an index, I, expressed as follows:

$$I = \frac{\text{moisture surplus} - \text{deficit}}{\text{potential evapotranspiration}} \times 100$$

If there is no surplus or deficit, the index is 0. Moist climates have positive indices, and dry climates negative. Thornthwaite, like Koeppen, gave his climate classes letter symbols. A, the "perhumid" moisture province, has an index of 100+; B, the humid province, corresponds to an index of 20 to 100; C, subhumid, 20 to -33; D, semiarid, -33 to -66; and E, the arid climates, indices of -66 to -100.

The island of Hawai'i is classified according to the Thornthwaite system in Figure 4.9. Note that perhumid A climates are typical of the windward (eastern) part of the island. Small areas of B, or humid climates, border the A climates, but most of the island is classified subhumid C or semiarid D.

In the Thornthwaite climatic classification, two areas of water surplus and two areas of deficit are identified on the Big Island (Figure 4.10). The areas with an annual water surplus exceeding 1,000 mm (40 in) comprise 20% (2,100 km² or 810 mi²) of the island, and are restricted to the high-rainfall regions

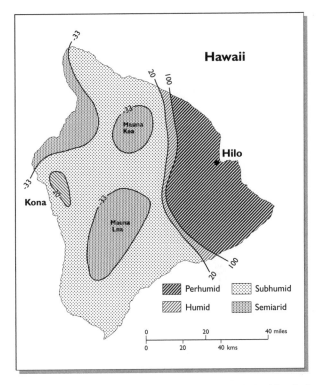

Figure 4.9 Thornthwaite climatic classification of the island of Hawai'i

of windward Mauna Kea, Mauna Loa, and the summit area of the Kohala Mountains. The annual surplus ranges as high as 3,377 mm (133 in) at middle elevations.

The area with an annual surplus between 0 and 1,000 mm (0–40 in) covers 21% (2,200 km² or 850 mi²) of the island, and extends from middle to high elevations on the windward slopes down to sea level. For the windward stations, there is typically a moderate summer dry period two to five months long.

The area with an annual deficit between 0 and 1,000 mm (0–40 in) comprises 54% (5,600 km² or 2,160 mi²) of the island, and includes the area predominantly leeward of Kohala, and the higher elevations of Mauna Kea and Mauna Loa. The dry period is concentrated in the summer on the

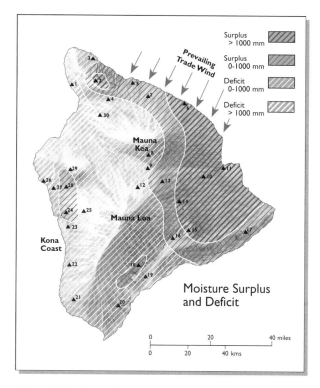

Surplus
> 1000 mm

Surplus
0-1000 mm

Deficit
0-1000 mm

Deficit
> 1000 mm

Figure 4.10 Areas of moisture surplus and deficit on the island of Hawai'i (after Juvik et al., 1978)

windward side and winter on the Kona side, and typically lasts six to twelve months.

The area with an annual deficit exceeding 1,000 mm (40 in), a zone of high moisture deficiency, comprises 5% (550 km² or 212 mi²) of the island, and is restricted to leeward Kohala and northern Kona. The annual moisture deficit may exceed 1,900 mm (75 in) in some areas.

The Thornthwaite climatic classification demonstrates graphically the tremendous climatic diversity on the island of Hawai'i. Although the Koeppen map showed only a relatively small portion of the island to be arid or semiarid, from the water balance

analysis it is evident that nearly 60% (the deficit zones above) of the island experiences an annual moisture deficit.

SUGGESTED READINGS

American Meteorological Society. 1951. On the rainfall of Hawaii: A group of contributions. *Meteorological Monographs* 1 (3): 1–55.

Ekern, P. C. Evapotranspiration patterns under trade wind weather regime on central Oahu. *Solar Energy* 11:1–9.

Ekern, P. C., and Chang, J. H. 1985. *Pan evaporation, State of Hawaii: 1894–1983.* Honolulu: Hawaii Dept. of Land and Natural Resources, Division of Water and Land Development (Report No. R74).

Giambelluca, T. W.; Lau, L. S.; Fok, Y. S.; and Schroeder, T. A. 1984. *Rainfall frequency study for Oahu.* Hawaii Dept. of Land and Natural Resources, Division of Water and Land Development (Report No. R73).

Giambelluca, T. W.; Nullet, M. A.; and Schroeder, T. A. 1986. *Rainfall atlas of Hawaii.* Honolulu: Hawaii Dept. of Land and Natural Resources, Division of Water and Land Development (Report No. R76).

Giambelluca, T. W.; Nullet, M. A.; Ridgley, M. A.; Eyre, P. R.; Moncur, J. E.; and Price, S. 1991. *Drought in Hawai'i.* Hawaii Dept. of Land and Natural Resources, Division of Water and Land Development (Report No. R88).

Juvik, J. O.; Singleton, D. C.; and Clarke, G. G. 1978. "Climate and water balance on the island of Hawaii." In *Mauna Loa Observatory,* ed. J. Miller, 129–139. Twentieth Anniversary Report, U.S. Dept. Commerce, NOAA Environmental Research Lab.

Meisner, B. N., and Schroeder, T. A. 1982. *Median rainfall: State of Hawaii.* Honolulu: Dept. of Land and Natural Resources, Division of Water and Land Development (Circular 88).

Taliaferro, W. J. 1959. *Rainfall of the Hawaiian Islands.* Honolulu: Hawaii Water Authority.

Thornthwaite, C. W. 1948. An approach toward a rational classification of climate. *Geographical Review* 38:55–94.

CHAPTER 5

Climate and Human Activity

In this chapter we discuss climate and human activity in the Hawaiian Islands. The climatic characteristics that make Hawai'i a beautiful place to visit, live, and work are described in the first section, followed by a discussion of climate and human comfort in Hawai'i. The negative human impact on air quality and recharge of groundwater is discussed in the next two sections. Section V outlines human use of wind and sun for energy in the Islands, and the final section concerns the development of the unique Hawaiian agriculture and its dependency on climate.

I. Hawai'i as a Place to Visit, Live, and Work   *Saul Price*

Hawai'i as a Place to Visit

Even today, with air travel making the whole world accessible, Hawai'i still evokes the exotic appeal spoken of by Mark Twain and continues to attract multitudes of visitors from every corner of the globe.

Between 1950 and 1992, the number of visitors staying overnight or longer in Hawai'i increased more than a hundredfold, from fewer than fifty thousand a year to more than six million, and their expenditures rose from $24 million to more than $6 billion per year. As a result, tourism has become the greatest contributor to the Hawaiian economy, exceeding military expenditures by three times. In contrast, during the period mentioned above, the resident population of Hawai'i only doubled, from about 500,000 to one million.

In the earlier years of that period, Hawai'i was a destination almost exclusively for the wealthy. Transport was by luxury liner from the West Coast of the United States—what Islanders refer to as "the Mainland." Hotels were few and costly and confined almost entirely to the Waikīkī area on O'ahu.

The present situation differs in almost every respect from that described above. The Islands are now served by many airlines, often offering reduced rates. So-called package deals, which include air fares, hotel accommodations, and often meals and side tours as well, have opened Hawai'i even to

73

those of modest means. At the same time, luxury resorts comparable to those found anywhere in the world have been built on all the islands. Hotels in Waikīkī have proliferated almost beyond counting, and recent development on the neighbor islands is enabling them to share in the tourist dollars.

The composition of the visitor population has also changed. While most of the tourists still come from the mainland U.S., many now arrive from Canada and Europe as well. And in recent years, honeymooners and other tourists from Japan have been arriving in such numbers that signs in hotels and shops are frequently in Japanese as well as in English.

Despite these changes, Hawai'i retains those qualities which have for so many years lured visitors from around the world: its natural beauty, with endless vistas of mountains and ocean, the ethnic variety of its people and their friendly "aloha spirit," and—perhaps most important of all—its unsurpassed climate. Since climate is the subject of this text, it will be the focus of our attention in what follows.

The reader will already understand from earlier chapters why the Hawaiian climate, with its fortunate coupling of ocean and landscape, has made these islands a perennial favorite. Hence, it will not be surprising that most visitors, especially those who arrive from cooler places or seasons, seek the sun and the sea, and that resorts therefore cluster along the sunny beaches, where the annual rainfall averages 635 mm (25 in) or less. In fact, the 635 mm (25 in) isohyet (line of equal rainfall), and in some places the 500 mm (20 in) isohyet, approximately delineate those favored sites. Almost without exception these sites are found on the southern and western coasts, leeward of the mountains relative to the prevailing trade winds (as we saw in Chapter 4).

Waikīkī Beach, on the southern coast of O'ahu, is the most famous visitor destination in the Islands, with more tourist hotels than the rest of the state combined. Each of the other islands, however, has its own clustering of resorts, constantly under expansion, with additional ones in the planning stage. Best known among these is the extremely dry and sunny Kona (leeward or western) Coast of the island of Hawai'i. On Maui, resort hotels congregate along the western coast of West Maui from Lahaina northward, and the southwestern coast of East Maui from Kīhei to Wailea. On Kaua'i, where Hurricane Iniki wreaked havoc with the resorts all over the island, a favored site is the Po'ipū area, on the island's southern coast. Moloka'i has a few resorts on its southern and western coasts, and Lāna'i, for the first time in its history, has recently acquired several elegant resort hotels.

Visitors to Hawai'i may seek—and find—such things as:

- Warm, sunny, trade wind weather suitable in every season for outdoor recreational activities, such as hiking, backpacking, golf, tennis, jogging, picnicking, sporting events, etc.
- Sunny beaches and year-round warm water, for sunbathing, swimming, surfing (body, board, and wind; Maui has been named the windsurfing capital of the world), snorkeling, scuba diving, fishing (from shore, reefs, small boats, and on the deep sea), biocollecting in estuaries and tidal pools, etc.
- Prevailing trade winds and moderate seas, for offshore and interisland boating, and recreational and competitive sailing.
- In some areas and times of year, waves suitable for world-class competitive surfing.
- Winter snow atop Mauna Kea, for the novelty of skiing in Hawai'i.
- Relatively small diurnal and seasonal variations in temperature, the absence of cold weather (except at high elevations) and other

climatic extremes, and the infrequency of prolonged hot spells and of severe or hazardous weather.

- An interesting and unusual climatic variety, with local differences in temperature, rainfall, wind, humidity, and vegetation, offering a wide choice of places to visit.
- Accessibility by car or on foot, within relatively short distances, of a diversity of scenic vistas and vegetation, ranging from sea level to high altitudes and from tropical rain forests to deserts and tundra.

Hawai'i as a Place to Live and Work

Obviously, the qualities that make Hawai'i appealing to visitors also make it an attractive place to live and work, and they may contribute to the fact that the population of Hawai'i has the longest average life expectancy of any state. In fact, the quality of the climate is probably of greater importance to the permanent resident, for whom it defines a way of life, than to casual visitors, most of whom remain for only a week or two.

One of the most pleasant and highly visible features of life in Hawai'i is an informality of dress appropriate to the tropical climate. Simple, lightweight clothing, including the colorful aloha shirt and *mu'umu'u,* is universally worn and considered acceptable for almost any social and even business occasion. Even in downtown Honolulu, occasional strollers in beachwear may be seen!

The climate also dictates the type of housing in Hawai'i. Most single-family residences are of light frame or frame and hollow tile single-wall construction, designed to take advantage of the natural ventilation provided by the prevailing trade winds. Large, overhanging eaves shelter the house interiors from all but the lowest sun, while trees and other plantings provide windbreaks and shade. An important part of many homes is the open *lānai* (the local term for a porch), often facing away from the trades, and in constant use throughout the year.

Air conditioning, although now widely used in hotels and in large office and apartment buildings, is a rarity in most homes. If it exists at all, it is usually confined to a window unit in a particular room. In fact, in most single-family dwellings, it would be difficult to close windows, louvers, and screened doors tightly enough to permit the practical use of air conditioning.

Many homes, however, have ceiling or portable floor fans for those sultry days of so-called Kona weather when the trade winds die down and warm humid air spreads over the Islands from offshore waters. If oppressive hot spells, like those of several summers in the mid 1980s, with daily maximum temperatures of 32 °C (90 °F) or higher for a week or more at a time, become increasingly frequent, window air conditioners may come into wider use.

Just as homes in Hawai'i are not designed for air conditioning, neither are they built for central heating. Most single-family dwellings are built on concrete slabs or on wooden posts slightly elevated above the ground. In fact, basements, where a heating plant might be accommodated, are a rarity. Central heating is rarely a necessity, with afternoon temperatures even in the coldest months seldom below 21 °C (70 °F) near sea level, and nighttime minimums rarely reaching 13 °C (the mid-50s). Only in a few localities at high elevations, like the Big Island's Volcano area, where nighttime temperatures occasionally drop to about 5 °C (the low 40s), might central heating be desirable. On the other hand, fireplaces are common in such places as the damp, cloudy upper valleys and cool heights on O'ahu overlooking Honolulu, and in similar areas on the other islands. Even there, however, they serve as much a social as a utilitarian purpose, and are used primarily on chilly winter nights.

II. Climate and Human Comfort   *Thomas Schroeder*

Thermal comfort may be defined as the absence of discomfort caused by heat or cold. A comfort zone is a range of conditions under which the thermoregulatory mechanisms of the body are least active. In Hawai'i, cold discomfort is seldom a problem, but heat discomfort can be.

The basic heat exchange equation for the human body is

$$Q = M \pm R \pm C - E$$

where Q = the body's change in heat content (measured as a change in core temperature); M = metabolism, the process by which food matter combines with oxygen in the body to produce heat; C = conduction and convection to or from the surroundings; R = radiation to or from the surroundings; and E = evaporation of perspiration (a cooling process).

Consider metabolic activity with R and C unaltered. The body produces perspiration. If the surrounding environment is sufficiently dry, the perspiration evaporates, cooling the body.

Various indices have been developed to evaluate the physiological effects of different climates. Table 6 shows relative comfort categories for several cities based on an effective temperature index devised by the American Society of Heating and Air Conditioning Engineers.

Humans build houses to protect themselves from extremes of the climate and to provide shelter. In Hawai'i, buildings are designed to keep the interiors cool. This is achieved principally by reflecting radiation from the sun, by insulation, by various methods of shading the structure, by ventilation, and by evaporatively cooling the surroundings. Reflecting radiation is achieved by choice of colors. White-painted surfaces exposed to the sun absorb only one-fifth as much heat as black-painted surfaces. This principle applies also to wall paint and roofing color. Insulation reduces the conductive heat transfer between the exterior walls or roof and the interior. This is achieved by materials selection, including thicker walls or roof, or by the use of intervening air layers as in a mid-latitude storm window. Overhanging roofs shade walls from the midday sun; window shades may be added. Trees shade houses very well. Surprisingly little wind, about 30 cm/sec (12 in/sec), is required for proper ventilation. This can be achieved by louvered doors or windows, or by means of ceiling fans. High-pitched roofs allow

Table 6 Relative Comfort Categories of Honolulu and Other Cities

Place	Comfort Category			
	Mild	Warm	Hot	Oppressively Hot
Manila			July–Aug.	May–June
Hong Kong	April, Nov.	May, Oct.	June–Sept.	
Bombay		Dec.–Feb.	Mar.–Apr. July–Nov.	May–June
Honolulu	Dec.–May	June–Nov.		
Los Angeles	July–Oct.			
Miami	Nov.–Apr.	May, Oct.	June–Sept.	
New York	June–Sept.			
Chicago	June–Sept.			

warm air to rise above the living areas. Finally, evaporative cooling is provided by surrounding the structure with water surfaces that evaporate or with vegetation that evapotranspires.

These architectural mechanisms have been used throughout history, in the Eskimo's igloo, the Hopi's cliff dwelling, and the Polynesian's grass shack. Unfortunately, as cities such as Honolulu have grown, crowded structures have reduced wind ventilation, while the need to keep out urban dirt and noise has forced architects to use the air conditioner.

Thermal comfort can also be influenced by clothing. Clothing for the Hawaiian climate should be light-colored to reduce solar heating, and loosely woven to permit air to circulate over the skin surface, enhancing conduction, convection, and evaporation. One interesting adaptation of thermal regulation is the gear chosen by marathon runners in Hawai'i. The runner bares as much of the body as legality or modesty allows. This enhances ventilation. The running singlet is designed to drain perspiration from the upper torso to the stomach. Here, the body's internal organs generate substantial heat, and evaporation of the accumulated perspiration cools this critical section of the body.

Evaporative cooling consumes the body's available water supply. As the supply becomes depleted, the core temperature rises progressively to the threshold of first uncomfortable heat exhaustion, followed by heatstroke. Heatstroke can be fatal unless immediately treated. As a general rule, a 5% loss of body weight during physical activity marks the threshold of heat exhaustion. So, drink plenty of water!

Almost everyone who visits Hawai'i wants to return home with a tan. Visitors should be aware, however, that the ultraviolet radiation that tans the skin can also cause painful sunburn and, for an unfortunate few, skin cancer. The exact burning mechanism is not well understood. It is believed to be a photochemical reaction by which an amino acid transforms into a substance which dilates the blood vessels. This substance causes reddening of the skin, blisters, and, in extreme cases, destruction of the skin with subsequent peeling. The burning rays seem to be restricted to wavelengths below .32 microns. Sunlight at slightly longer wavelengths, between .32 and .40 microns, transforms a different amino acid into melanin. Melanin colors and protects the skin from the shorter-wavelength ultraviolet rays. Sun block lotions of protection factor 15 or more, if used properly, protect the skin from most harmful effects.

Under clear skies, the amount of ultraviolet radiation penetrating the atmosphere is determined by the sun's elevation above the horizon. A change in solar elevation from 40° to 60° nearly doubles the amount of ultraviolet radiation. Since Hawai'i lies within the tropics, the sun angle remains high year-round, ranging at noon from 45° in winter to 90° in summer. Ultraviolet radiation also increases with altitude. With a 60° sun angle, the ultraviolet radiation at the summit of Mauna Loa is about 50% greater than at sea level.

III. Air Quality in Hawai'i   *Thomas Schroeder*

The U.S. Environmental Protection Agency defines air pollution as "the presence in the ambient air of substances put there by man or nature in concentrations sufficient to interfere directly or indirectly with comfort, safety, health or with the full use or enjoyment of property." Source emissions and atmospheric conditions control pollution concentration. In Hawai'i, the trade winds provide ventilation that maintains low concentrations at most locations. Nevertheless, local problems and a few general problems not widely recognized do exist. Board of

Health statistics indicate that respiratory problems affect 15% of the population, although these include numerous allergies to the innumerable flowering plants and fungi that thrive in Hawai'i.

Volcanoes are the biggest polluters in the state. Kīlauea emits copious quantities of sulfur compounds and rare toxic gases, such as mercury vapor. The caldera of Kīlauea and eruptive vents in the rift zones liberate sulfur dioxide, a major source of respiratory distress and eye irritation. Sulfur dioxide reacts with water vapor to produce sulfuric acid, which is one of the two major sources of acid rain. Low temperature emissions at steam vents are sources of hydrogen sulfide. In low amounts, hydrogen sulfide produces an odor similar to rotten eggs, but in high concentrations it can be lethal. Since geothermal wells emit hydrogen sulfide, the developers of geothermal power plants proposed for the Hawaiian volcano sites must plan for hydrogen sulfide abatement.

During eruptive phases on the Big Island, volcanic haze envelops regions downwind of the vents, and the Kona sea-breeze circulation traps pollutants. When southerly winds coincide with an eruption, the plume drifts to the more northerly islands. The haze builds with time, as land and sea breezes recycle the particles and gases daily. Major eruptions such as those experienced at Mauna Loa in 1950 and 1984 liberate plumes that cover wide areas of the Pacific. The 1950 Mauna Loa plume drifted southwest via the trade winds, and then apparently was carried by the upper westerlies back to Honolulu. The 1984 Mauna Loa plume reached the Philippines in twelve days. Prolonged eruptions have damaged crops near the vents.

Generally, volcanic emissions are a problem only near the source. In June 1987, Kīlauea erupted for 340 consecutive days, yet volcanic smog (called vog) seldom appeared at Honolulu 400 km (250 mi) to the northwest. Furthermore, volcanic pollution cannot be controlled. Hawai'i fortunately lacks heavy "smokestack" industries, but in cities like Honolulu, automobiles cause most of the pollution. In 1972, carbon monoxide concentrations at the primary monitoring site in Honolulu surpassed the state clean air standards more than fifty times. By 1979 the number had declined to ten. In the same period, annual mean concentrations dropped by two-thirds. Improved automobile emission controls no doubt contributed to these reductions. During Kona weather, the combination of vehicle and power plant emissions causes a haze layer to form over the city.

When the Hawaiian electric utilities burn oil, its sulfuric content is emitted as sulfur dioxide. Sulfur dioxide emissions are of concern near the plants, although emission controls have been implemented with guidance from the Environmental Protection Agency. New generators are required to burn low-sulfur oil. The utilities and the EPA have explored the concept that certain types of weather (e.g., fresh trade winds) might allow the burning of medium-sulfur oil. This issue is unresolved as of this writing, but the utility customer could realize significant savings if a shift to medium-sulfur oil were possible.

Some agricultural practices also pollute the air. Both the sugar and pineapple industries use burning as an effective step in the crop cycle. Sugar planters burn the fields prior to harvest, and pineapple growers burn to prepare for the next planting. These fires produce large smoke plumes containing particulates that fall out downwind, causing those individuals who live downwind to complain of respiratory distress. Although the state has developed standards for "burn" and "no burn" days, complaints have continued. In the central valley of Maui, the Maui Vortex (see Chapter 2) traps smoke from agricultural fires and local power plants. A study of cane fires in the early 1970s found that much of the particulate matter collected in sampling equipment downwind of the fires was silicate. Silicate is the primary constituent of soil. Apparently, the fire behaves as a small fire storm, and as the air rises in the heated updraft, inflowing air picks up surface soil and carries it aloft. The fate of agricultural burning is one of several issues to be resolved as Hawai'i seeks to improve the quality of its air.

Hawai'i is far from major continental land masses, yet pollutants travel great distances to the Islands. Dust from the great deserts of Asia has been detected at the Mauna Loa Observatory on the Big Island. Hawaiian rainwater, furthermore, has been found to be acidic. National Oceanic and Atmospheric Administration researchers John Miller (Air Resources Laboratory, Silver Spring, Maryland) and Alan Yoshinaga (Mauna Loa Observatory, Hilo, Hawai'i) have documented a case of acid rain in the Hawaiian Islands. Since 1974, they have analyzed more than 1,700 rainwater samples collected at nine sites on the island of Hawai'i, at altitudes from sea level to 3,400 m (11,150 ft). Most of the rain collected was acid rain, according to the rule that acid rain has a pH below 5.6—the pH of pure water acidified by atmospheric carbon dioxide. ("pH" is a system used to specify the range of acidity and alkalinity of different substances. A pH of 7 is neutral: acids have pH values less than 7 and alkaline substances have pH values greater than 7.) The pH of rain, they found, decreased with increasing altitude, averaging 5.2 at sea level and 4.3 at 2,500 m (8,200 ft). The average annual pH in the northeastern United States is also about 4.3. The observed pH in the Hawai'i samples ranged from about 3.7 to 5.7.

Miller and Yoshinaga found that the primary acid in the rain was sulfuric acid, but they could not find an adequate source (including volcanoes) on any of the Islands. They set up a collection site on the island of Kaua'i, 500 km (310 mi) northwest of the island of Hawai'i. Kaua'i has a smaller population

and has no active volcanoes. Even so, the average annual pH at the site was 4.8, the same as at a Big Island site at the same altitude.

Measurements from thirty years ago on the windward slopes of Hawai'i had pH values of about 5. Recent measurements on the slopes of Hawai'i and leeward slopes of O'ahu had median pH values from 4.2 to 4.5. In the immediate vicinity of Kīlauea, pH values were from 3 to 3.5, and these values spread as far as O'ahu during eruptive phases. It can be concluded that Hawai'i, although far removed from major industrial sources of acidity, does experience acid rain, probably from a combination of periodic vulcanism, upwind oceanic upwelling, and the transport of continental dust via the jet stream.

IV. Climate and Groundwater   *Tom Giambelluca*

The Hawaiian Islands are totally dependent on rainfall scavenged from the trade winds by the rugged topography to supply all the water needs of agriculture, industry, and domestic consumption. Even for islands so blessed with abundant rainfall, water supply is becoming a critically limited resource in some areas. The pressures of population growth have made water shortage an increasingly frequent problem. Agricultural and urban development alter the landscape, not only increasing the demand for water but also changing the water balance and causing water contamination. Thus, both the supply of water and the quality of water are affected. In southern O'ahu, where the largest concentration of population in Hawai'i resides, the various water supply problems facing Hawai'i are of most concern. Here the climatic diversity and the mosaic of human activity have tremendous impacts on the water supply.

Because of the geology and topography of the

island, surface water on Oʻahu is relatively difficult to exploit, and groundwater is the main water resource. Since the island's first well was drilled in 1879, the water table has declined by more than 4 m (13 ft) in some places, a reduction of about 40% of the original volume of stored water. Many coastal wells have become salty as seawater has replaced the retreating freshwater. With increasing demand for water, questions have been raised concerning the safe limit of water extraction from the important aquifers of the Pearl Harbor–Honolulu basin (Figure 5.1). The limit ultimately depends on the rate of groundwater recharge (the amount of fresh water annually reaching the water table). But with changing land use, the recharge rate, and thus the limits to safe use of the aquifers, are also changing.

The pattern of groundwater recharge in southern Oʻahu reflects the diversity of climate. Ignoring the effects of land use, the distribution of recharge, shown in Figure 5.2, closely resembles the rainfall distribution. A maximum recharge of nearly 6,000 mm/yr (235 in/yr) occurs in the northeast corner of the basin, near the Koʻolau crest. Recharge dimin-

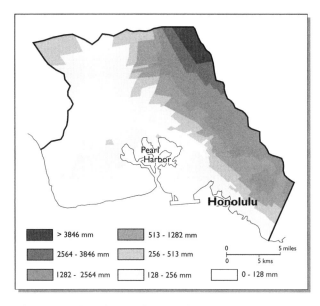

Figure 5.2 Natural groundwater recharge pattern in the Pearl Harbor–Honolulu Basin

ishes rapidly toward the leeward lowlands, where annual recharge averages less than 125 mm (5 in). The important area of natural recharge is clearly confined to the leeward Koʻolau slopes.

The present land use pattern (Figure 5.3) is a diverse mixture of growing urban development and shrinking areas of sugarcane, pineapple, and forest. Different land uses imply differing amounts of water demand. The influence of land use is also reflected in the recharge pattern shown in Figure 5.4. Sugarcane irrigation and suppression of evapotranspiration from pineapple fields result in significant recharge areas in drier portions of the region. Urbanization, which affects the water balance by increasing runoff, decreasing evapotranspiration, and adding water through lawn sprinkling, results in higher recharge in some areas and lower in others compared with the natural rate.

Human activities greatly affect the hydrology of southern Oʻahu. The total basin recharge prior to

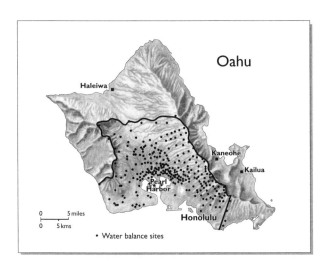

Figure 5.1 Pearl Harbor–Honolulu basin aquifer

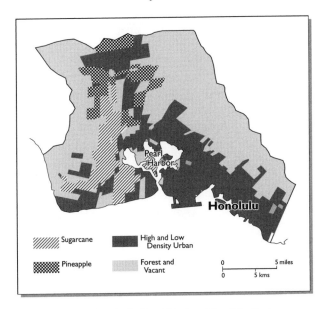

Figure 5.3 Land use in the Pearl Harbor–Honolulu Basin

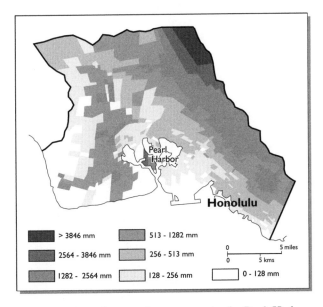

Figure 5.4 Groundwater recharge pattern in the Pearl Harbor–Honolulu Basin including the effects of land use

large-scale urban development was about 14.7 m³/sec (484 ft³/sec). Today it is 17.0 m³/sec (557 ft³/sec), a 15% increase. Most of that increase can be attributed to sugarcane irrigation and evapotranspiration suppression by pineapple. Land use is changing in the central part of the basin. Sugarcane is being replaced by residential development, which demands less water but also returns less of it to the groundwater. New housing on former pineapple lands uses more water and provides less recharge than before. Overall, conversion of land from agricultural to urban use lowers the safe groundwater withdrawal rate of the basin.

In confronting the future water supply problems in Hawai'i, planners must be cognizant of the implied water supply and demand characteristics of the changing landscape. They should recognize that the impacts of land use change on the hydrologic cycle depend also on climate. The influence of climate should always be considered when making decisions concerning regional development alternatives.

Groundwater Contamination

While saltwater encroachment has long been the major source of groundwater contamination on O'ahu, trace quantities of several toxic organic chemicals discovered in well water have raised serious concerns. In central O'ahu, contamination by dibromochloropropane (DBCP), ethylene dibromide (EDB), and trichloropropane (TCP) forced the temporary closing of several drinking-water wells because of suspected health risks. DBCP and EDB are pesticides, and TCP is an impurity of another pesticide formerly used in pineapple cultivation in the Islands. It is suspected that DBCP and TCP were leached from the soils of pineapple fields by downward-percolating water, eventually reaching the groundwater in measurable concentrations. Because EDB is also a constituent of leaded gasoline, its source is uncertain; it may have come from fuel pipeline leaks.

Prior to discovery of agrochemical contamination, it was believed that the use of pesticides in this region posed no threat to the groundwater. It was thought unlikely that any significant residues, because of their high volatility, would percolate through hundreds of meters of soil and rock to the groundwater. As previously noted, however, pineapple fields cause higher recharge than natural surfaces by suppressing evapotranspiration, and thus the discovery of contamination is not surprising. The accelerated leaching resulting from the higher recharge obviously makes contamination of this kind more likely under pineapple cultivation. The spatial pattern of contamination shows the highest concentrations of DBCP and TCP near the wettest pineapple fields, where recharge is relatively high. This observation underlines the importance of climate in the groundwater contamination process.

V. Wind and Solar
Energy   *Thomas Schroeder*

It has been shown in Chapters 2 and 3 that the Islands have reliable wind and solar radiation regimes; these energy resources were exploited early in the post-discovery years. Windmills were used for pumping water, and solar water heaters were constructed in Honolulu as early as 1930. More recently, the development of centralized power systems has made these energy sources less desirable and their use has waned.

State officials realized that the Islands' physical isolation made the almost exclusively oil-fired electric systems vulnerable to discontinuities in the fuel supply. Hawai'i also pays a premium for electricity because of added shipping charges. The energy crisis of 1973 awakened the residents of Hawai'i to the precarious status of their energy supply. Among numerous alternate energy sources examined by state and utility officials were wind and solar energy.

Humans have employed wind as an energy source for millennia. Wind has long been used to pump water, and more recently to generate electricity. The basic wind energy conversion system (WECS) consists of an electric generator driven by the energy extracted from a blade turning in the wind. The blade technology is similar to that of a helicopter rotor. Since wind is a diffuse energy source, large blade areas are required to extract useful amounts of energy. The 200kw MOD-OA WECS that was run experimentally at Kahuku, O'ahu in 1981 had a blade diameter of 38 m (125 ft). The power produced was sufficient for 100 households.

Figure 5.5 depicts the performance of a typical WECS as a function of wind speed. The WECS produces power over a limited range of wind speeds, and produces what is termed rated power (Pr) over an even more limited range. At low ranges there is inadequate energy to turn the generator; at high speeds, blade damage may occur.

Climatology is a major consideration in assessing the economic viability of WECS installations. The energy available from the wind varies by a factor

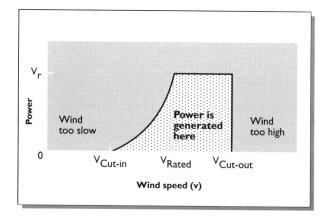

Figure 5.5 Wind energy conversion system performance

equal to the cube of the wind speed. A 10% increase in wind speed corresponds to a 33% increase in available energy. Average wind speed alone is not an adequate estimate, however, and detailed information about the statistical distribution of wind speeds at a site is necessary. From these statistics, economic analyses can be carried out.

Wind energy maps for the Hawaiian Islands are presented in Figure 5.6. These are based on field measurements, climatological data, and physical reasoning. The maps resemble the speed distribution expected under trade wind conditions. Since the trades blow on 70% of all days, they should be the major power producers. The high-wind areas are at the corners of the Islands, the crests of lower mountain ridges, and the lower saddles between large mountains.

The MOD-OA turbine experiment at Kahuku on the northeast tip of O'ahu was the most successful experimental wind program ever conducted by the U.S. Department of Energy. In the first seven months of operation the power output averaged 149 kW, a capacity factor of 74.5, almost double that of all other experimental sites. Encouraged by the success of the MOD-OA, Hawaiian Electric Company has installed a "wind farm" of fifteen 600-kW units on a series of ridges near the original MOD-OA site (Figure 5.7). This is still an experiment, since the total of 9 MW is a minor fraction of O'ahu's 900 MW demand for electricity.

In 1987, the Department of Energy and Hawaiian Electric Industries erected the world's largest experimental wind turbine at the old MOD-OA site at Kahuku. This behemoth has a blade diameter of 80 m (262 ft) and generates 3.2 MW of electricity. The generator has successfully functioned through its experimental period, and it is now connected to the O'ahu electric grid.

The Big Island also has wind farms. The peak electricity demand on the island of Hawai'i is only 75 MW, and wind can have a substantial impact. A large array of small WECS (198 units @ 17 kW) at Kahua Ranch in northwest Hawai'i can provide 4.5% (3.4 MW) of the island's peak load. Kahua is one of the windiest documented wind-energy sites in the United States. Two smaller farms on the island produce nearly 2 MW of energy. Mitsubishi Corporation of Japan has developed an additional wind farm at South Point (Ka Lae), the southern tip of the island. A number of private individuals who own small turbines sell their excess electricity to add to the Big Island electric grid. Penetration of wind energy into the electric supply on the Big Island is approaching the limits that systems planners desire, since wind is a fluctuating power source. Too much wind energy may impair the quality of network electricity, with disastrous effects upon sensitive electronic equipment.

Wind farm planning has progressed slowly on Maui and Moloka'i, and the 1987 relaxation in oil prices has further slowed the pace of development. However, interest remains high, especially on Maui.

Solar Energy

Since solar radiation is responsible for the temperature contrasts that produce it, wind is an *indirect* manifestation of solar radiation. Solar energy denotes energy *directly* derived from solar radiation. In Hawai'i, solar energy is used to heat water and generate electricity. Solar water heaters consist of black-painted copper or aluminum tubing protected by a plexiglass cover. Water within the tubing is heated by absorbed sunlight and the heat is transferred through the highly conductive tube. The hot water is then either pumped or syphoned to a storage tank for future use.

Solar energy is diffuse. The sunlight falling on a square meter of a collector on one of the Islands, if completely converted to electricity, could power only

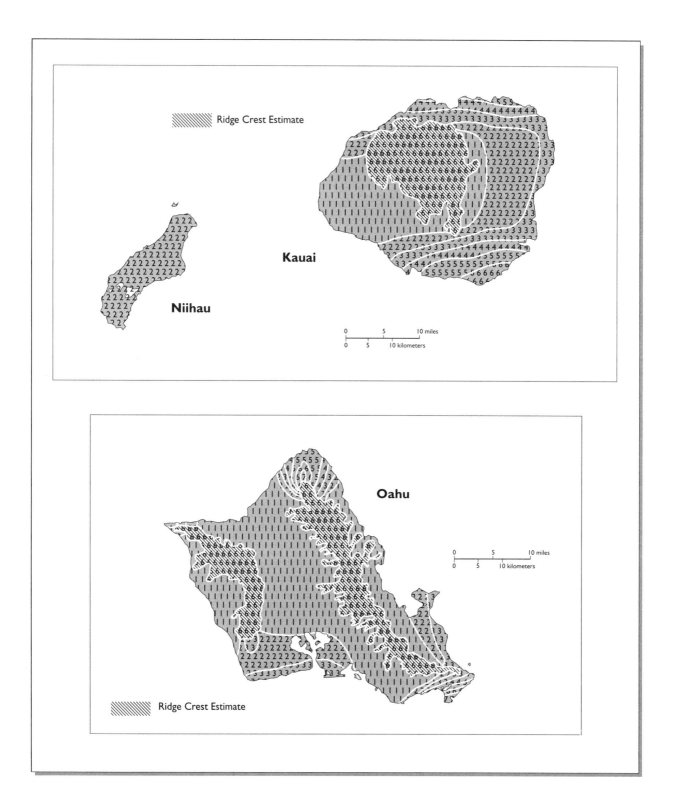

Figure 5.6 Estimated annual wind energy for the Hawaiian Islands (after Schroeder and Hovi, 1980) (left) Kauaʻi County, Honolulu

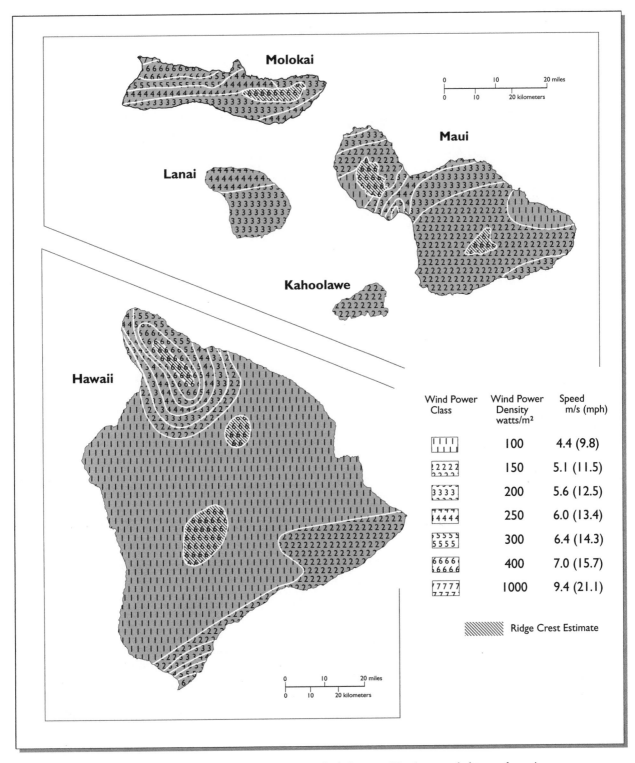

County and (right) Maui County and Hawai'i County Average annual wind power. (Numbers are wind power classes.)

Figure 5.7 Boeing Mod-5 3.2 megawatt-wind energy conversion system: the world's largest wind turbine

radiation. A substantial amount of the light from the sky is diffuse radiation scattered by atmospheric constituents, and it cannot be focused.

Photovoltaic cells convert sunlight directly into electricity. Costs of these systems have been decreasing, and solar-powered watches and calculators are common. In Hawai'i, photovoltaics have been installed in residential demonstration projects, and also have been used to power remote weather stations throughout the state. In these instances, the photovoltaics cost less than installation of electric power lines. During Hurricane Iwa a critical weather station on Kaua'i functioned perfectly throughout the storm, although the data were lost by failure of the telephone system, which normally carries the data to the central weather office at Līhu'e. The telephone system failed when the electric utility lines blew down.

Wind and solar energy have contributed to the Islands' power supply, although the current relaxation of oil prices has slowed development. Nevertheless, the continued vulnerability to energy supply interruption in Hawai'i encourages alternate energy development.

VI. Climate and Agriculture   Paul Ekern

Agriculture utilizes sunlight to manufacture useful plant products through photosynthesis; hence, sunlight is the major determinant of the yield potential of a site. Actual yield depends on the display of chlorophyll by a plant, on temperature for the rate of reactions, on water as the primary plant constituent (more realistically on the water balance among rainfall and irrigation, evapotranspiration, runoff, and percolation), and finally on wind, which transports momentum, carbon dioxide, heat, dust, insects, and disease organisms to and from plants.

In the Hawaiian Islands, the natural plant cover

a few light bulbs. Even so, the simplest solar water heaters (flat plate collectors) have proven successful in Hawai'i. They have been installed even in rainy climates such as Hilo, where the diurnal variation of cloud and rain is such that at midday (the high-sun hours), skies are often clear enough to allow water heating.

Concentrating collectors that employ parabolic mirrors to concentrate the energy have not fared as well. A parabolic dish can focus only direct-beam which formed before the advent of humans was changed by the early Hawaiian agriculturists as they selected and tended preferred plants appropriate to the particular climatic zone. Their agronomic practices were suited to subsistence production of the fundamentals of food, fiber, and fuel. Drastic change again occurred with the onset of Western agricultural practices, in which products were sold to provide funds for financial operations (a parallel to the cash crop production of most of today's tropical agricultural systems). Agricultural research in the Islands now explores the possibility of new specialty items such as macadamia nuts, cacao, and hybrid seed corn, products that must compete for sunlight with the tourist industry's "fun in the sun" image.

Today, as in the past, plant associations invade the basaltic lava flows and eruption debris to occupy the different climatic zones to which the plants must adapt in response to sunlight, water balance, and temperature. The plant associations that were formed in Hawai'i prior to humans' arrival have been hypothesized by various methods. Achieving a relative state of equilibrium depended on the arrival of fewer than 200 plant species, faunal predators that did *not* include grazing mammals, subsequent volcanic eruptions, and the passage of time required for adaptation and the spread of species. A key limitation to plant growth was the paucity of nitrogen-fixing legumes, other than the forest trees such as 'ōhi'a lehua, koa, māmane, and the dry-forest wiliwili. It is uncertain whether the mycorrhizal fungi so critical to phosphorus utilization arrived with the early trees. With no grazing predators, the original plant associations remained fragile and defenseless against the later arrival of goats and cattle. These plant associations in turn played a large part in forming the soils on which they grew.

The relative seasonal uniformity of sunlight, that prime determinant of yield potential, is seen in the fact that a clear winter day receives only 15% less energy than a clear summer day (as we saw in Chapter 3). Variation in cloudiness, however, causes an average winter day to receive 30% less sunlight than an average summer day in Honolulu. Topography so distorts the rainfall and cloudiness that the rainy interiors of the Islands receive only one-third as much sunshine as the surrounding ocean. An example of crop response to sunlight is found in the fact that yields of maize from summer plantings at Waimānalo on the Windward Coast of O'ahu are twice those of winter plantings.

In summer in the Hawaiian latitude, the noonday sun is directly overhead and there is little difference in sunlight on north- or south-facing slopes. But in winter, when the solar elevation is only 45°, the sun shines beneath the cloud decks deeply into south-facing valleys, which thus have more sunlight in December than in June. Sugarcane in winter had twice the growth of vegetative tillers on a sunny 10% south face than on a similar cooler north slope. The drier, sunnier south-facing valley slopes are grass-covered, while trees dominate the cooler, moister north-facing slopes.

Day length influences the amount of sunlight, as well as governing the onset of flowering for many crops. Even the shortest winter day of 10.8 hours or the longest summer day of 13.3 hours does not have the extreme dark periods needed for the photoperiodic response of many temperate-latitude plants. As a consequence, sugarcane varieties can be selected for Hawai'i which will not flower, but remain vegetative for two or even three years of growth, thus increasing sucrose production. Pineapple too will normally remain vegetative. The plants, however, can be forced to flower with the application of chemicals so that the entire field ripens simultaneously. Subtle though it may be, the combination of day length change, moisture status, and temperature is sufficient to cause seasonality of growth and flowering, as exemplified by the patterns for many trees introduced into Hawaiian forests.

Air temperature controls the rate of many plant growth processes. (For example, the length of the local winter vegetative period of maize growth is 50% longer than the summer period at Waimānalo.) We noted the marked uniformity of Hawaiian air temperature through the year in Chapter 3. Measurements have shown that temperatures for bare soil at 8–15 cm (about 3–6 in) depth average more than 1 °C (2 °F) warmer in winter and 3 °C (5 °F) warmer in summer than the shelter height air temperature, which averages 26.7 °C (80 °F) near sea level. Beneath an insulative trash mulch or a live plant canopy, however, soil temperatures are identical to average air temperatures. Beneath a plant canopy, soil temperatures decrease approximately at the dry adiabatic rate of 6.5 °C/km (3.6 °F/1,000 ft) from sea level to the cloud base at about 600 m (2,000 ft). (See Figure 3.10.)

Although the average temperatures near sea level approximate the optimum for temperate-latitude plants, they are below the optimum of 30–33 °C (85–90 °F) for tropical grasses such as maize and sugarcane. At 300 m (1,000 ft) elevation, winter soil temperatures are only 20 °C (68 °F), and pineapple root growth and nutrient uptake are half the rate of the warm summer period. A black plastic mulch is used for pineapple production, since it increases soil temperatures nearly 6 °C (10 °F) and can double the potential growth rate. Similarly, an insulative trash mulch that might conserve water against evaporation can be used only for low-lying areas, since the temperature reduction for the cooler upland areas promotes root rot, which destroys the less-tolerant pineapple rootlets.

Midlatitude vegetables and flowers can grow in the cooler zones above 600 m (2,000 ft), though at higher elevations frost can be a hazard. Winter snow on occasion blankets the top of Haleakalā, and snowdrifts persist into July on the peaks of Mauna Loa and Mauna Kea. Patterned ground from frost heave and permafrost, perhaps a relict from the mountain glacier of some 12,000 years ago, still exists in the cindery top of Mauna Kea near Lake Waiau. It should be noted that the growth of midlatitude legumes such as ladino clover in upland pastures is strongly seasonal and thus limits the potential for winter grazing.

Over the open ocean, there is a net annual water deficit of about 1,200 mm (47 in) between the rainfall of approximately 700 mm (28 in) and evaporation of 1,900 mm (75 in). In addition, island topography profoundly alters the balance among rainfall, evaporation, percolation, and runoff. Annual potential evapotranspiration on the cloudy uplands can be less than 500 mm (20 in), but becomes more than 2,500 mm (100 in) with positive advection on the hot, dry leeward plains. These sunny plains, with a potential annual water deficit of 735 mm (29 in), are normally barren but can be made highly productive by heavy irrigation. Beneath the trade wind inversion, cloudiness decreases the net radiation available for evaporation, but in the dry sunny zones at higher elevations, evaporation potential again rises to that near sea level, and vegetation is almost nonexistent.

Agriculture must defend the soil against the kinetic energy of falling raindrops, which provide the initial power for erosion. Trade wind warm rainfall has smaller drop sizes; hence the summer rainfall erosion hazard is usually slight. Thunderstorm rainfall from spring and fall weather systems, which contain large drops, has high kinetic energy. Careful crop planning is required, since the annual erosional hazards are as severe as any in the continental United States.

Island topography interacts with the winds to accentuate velocities on ridge crests and island corners. Wind erosion, which is proportional to wind power and thus to the cube of wind velocity, is enhanced on dry soil. Mechanical damage, often accompanied by salt spray observed near coastal sites, has been used to provide an index of the direction and relative power of the wind in the Islands. Many Hawaiian areas require shelter belt protection both for the soil and the growing crop.

Some Island areas, in the lee of the prevailing summer trade winds, experience very light winds as the wind flow weakens after crossing the ridge. This results in low evaporation, with dew as often as 250 nights of the year, and leaf blight and other disease problems as a consequence of the high frequency of wetted leaf surfaces. Where the major mountain masses such as Mauna Loa and Mauna Kea project through the stabilizing trade wind inversion, the winds are diverted and land-sea breeze circulations are enhanced by lee side slope flow, as we saw in Chapter 2. Midday cloudiness and the summer rainfall maximum resulting from sea breeze circulation on the Kona Coast of Hawai'i have been exploited for coffee production, without the need for the more usual shade canopy found in most coffee producing areas.

The soils which developed from the interaction of plants with the rather uniform volcanic rock provide indirect indices of the climatic provinces in Hawai'i. Current soil classification names incorporate the water balance and temperature regimes that are described in Chapter 4. Thus the soil map groups the climatic provinces with the natural vegetation zone, and indicates the agricultural potential. However, caution must be used in interpreting these maps, for topsoil takes perhaps 1,000 years/in to form, and dramatic climate changes have occurred in Hawai'i in the last 5,000 to 10,000 years, the length of time necessary for a typical depth of topsoil to form. The highland bogs of Kaua'i, Maui, and Moloka'i reflect the change in water regime and plant cover that occurred as temperatures increased

some 13,000 years ago, the glacial ice melted, and sea level rose to reach its current levels about 6,000 years ago. Not only were former coastal plains flooded, but changes in the strength and position of the circumpolar westerly jet stream increased the intercontinental transport of quartz- and potassium-bearing illite dust which reached the Island soils.

This natural background set the stage for the arrival of the Hawaiians, who, about 1,300 years ago, brought new plants and agronomic practices to the Islands and inadvertently hastened soil erosion.

For the first 500 years, their hunting and gathering economy near the coastal regions was augmented by slash-and-burn, shifting agriculture on the talus (debris) slopes of the rainy windward valleys. Erosion from the talus filled the valley bottoms, and paddy culture of taro was later developed on the alluvium. The eroded talus uplands were terraced and used for dryland taro, sweet potato, and some yam cultivation. Sugarcane, banana, and breadfruit were also introduced but were not systematically planted. The Hawaiians' subsistence agronomy for production of food, fiber, and fuel required only minimal cultural inputs. No draft animals were available for tillage or harvest, and only green manures were used for fertilizer. No pea or bean plants were grown, and probably only bluegreen algae fixed nitrogen to sustain crop growth.

Taro, the new staple crop, had a low potential response to sunlight, low efficiency of carbon dioxide use, and a relatively low temperature optimum. Not only was the leaf very sensitive to water stress, but excessive irrigation was required to cool the corm and reduce root rot. Intricate ditch systems were developed to supply water for irrigation. This need for flowing water beyond the need of evapotranspiration alone has brought continued dispute over allocation of water rights for traditional taro culture in Hawai'i.

The Hawaiians used the dry forest uplands for

the culture of sweet potato and yam by carefully husbanding the naturally available moisture with mulches for these drought-tolerant plants. The native rain forest was probably little used. Since charcoal was not manufactured, use of the native rain forest for firewood and timber became significant only after the advent of Western agriculture. Fire was employed extensively in the lowland dry forest to encourage the growth of pili grass, which was used as house thatch.

The Hawaiians brought chicken, pig, and dog, potential protein sources, from their Polynesian roots. A number of the large, endemic flightless birds became extinct under hunting pressures. The major protein supply came from fishing on the coral reefs. Near-shore areas were enclosed as ponds to raise fish as a ready meat source. The use of the land by the early Hawaiians on the Big Island is shown in Figure 5.8.

The Hawaiian Classification of Vegetation Zones

The Hawaiian names for the vegetative zones in the Islands described their agricultural potential. The term *kua* (back) described the mountain zones: *kuahiwi* (backbone), for the central mountains and *kualono*, the broad ridges or peaks. *Kuamauna* (back mountain) described the rounded Moanalua mountain slopes, and below this was the *kuahea*, the cold and misty *māmane-nīao* zone. The orographic cloud zone was *wao* (uplands), the uppermost forested subzone *wao nahele* (wilderness), and the *wao nahele ma'ukele* were the wet, muddy uplands where the monarchs of the forest grew. Below this were the *wao akua* (uplands of the spirits), followed by the *wao kanaka* (the uplands of man), where the *'ama'u* tree fern grew and where the uppermost zone of cultivation invaded the lower reaches of the rain forest. Narrow bands just below the *wao* zones were named *'āpa'a* (hard and baked), *'ilima* (where 'ilima, the lei

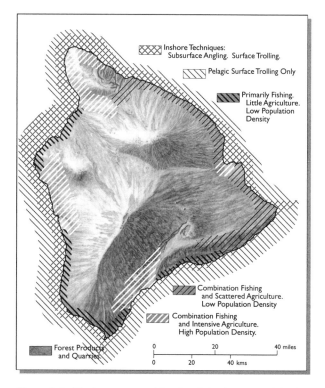

Figure 5.8 Maximum sea and land exploitation zones, island of Hawai'i, 1778 (from T. Stell Newman, "Hawaiian Fishing and Farming on the Island of Hawai'i in A.D. 1778." Dept. of Land and Natural Resources, Division of State Parks, Honolulu, Hawai'i, 1968. Copyright by T. Stell Newman 1968 Lapakahi Research Contract.)

of the ali'i, grew), and the *pahe'e* zone with grass for sliding. The *kula* (dry plains) extended from the edge of the rain forest to the seacoast. Uppermost was the *kula uka* (inland plain), then the *kula waena* (middle plain), and finally the *kula kai* (sea plain). The *kahakai* (seashore) was too dry for cultivation and was used largely for dwellings. A table summarizing these zones is given below (Table 7).

The lower part of the *kula kai* zone was used for taro. In 1884 *kula* was legally defined as land above the reach of *'auwai* (irrigation ditches and the lower areas of wetlands designated taro lands). These cor-

Table 7 Hawaiian Agricultural Zones: Kona Coast, Hawai'i

Zone	Elevation	Annual Rainfall	Crops
Kahakai	0–750′	below 50″	living zone, small gardens of sweet potatoes and coconuts
Kula kai	750–1,800′	30–60″	breadfruit, some sweet potato, wauke
Kula uka	1,000–2,500′	60–80″	sweet potato, dryland taro, wauke
Wao	2,500–4,000′	80–100″	bananas and plantains just below and within forest

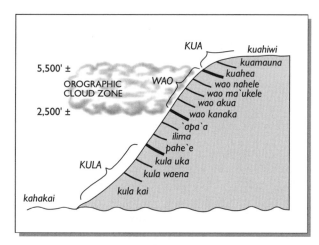

Figure 5.9 Hawaiian classification of vegetation (from Na Makani O Moanalua Vol. VI [3], 1980. Moanalua Garden Foundation Inc., 1352 Pineapple Place, Honolulu. Two-page mimeo sheet. Hawaiian names as used by David Malo.)

responded to the *kahawai* (place of fresh water) valleys where steams were diverted through *auwai* into the taro patches. The maximum land exploitation zones for the island of Hawai'i shown in Figure 5.9 are remarkably similar to those currently exploited by today's agriculture.

The Impact of Western Culture

After European contact in the late 1700s, goats, sheep, and cattle (grazers and browsers) were introduced to Hawai'i, upsetting the natural vegetation balance. Feral goats, and for a time feral cattle, devastated the fragile plant systems, which had only meager defense mechanisms. The European boar crossed with the smaller Polynesian pig, and this larger, more aggressive animal rooted in the island rain forest with dire results. Rice succeeded taro on many paddies, while small grains and potatoes were grown without irrigation, particularly in the mid-1800s when an export market developed in the western United States. Soon, however, traditional tropical plantation production prevailed, with cash crops such as sugarcane (similar to the farming systems that dominated other colonial tropics). The early Hawaiians had grown some sugarcane, but major engineering works such as the East Maui irrigation ditch in 1878 permitted the large-scale diversion of water from the rainy windward slopes to the dry, sunny leeward plains where sugarcane was grown. Discovery of artesian groundwater beneath the Ewa–Waipahu plain on O'ahu led to explosive development of irrigated sugarcane culture in the dry forest climate zones, little used by the early Hawaiians.

This sugarcane, a tropical grass from the riverine banks of Southeast Asia, has unique properties that make it ideal for irrigation. These four-carbon tropical grasses use carbon dioxide more efficiently than the three-carbon plants, and yield more in response to both high sunlight and high temperature. Highest yield requires as much as 2,500 mm (100 in) of annual irrigation, as well as large inputs of fossil fuel in the form of fertilizers, herbicides, pesticides, and machine power for tillage and harvest operations. The combination of day length and temperature in the critical mid-September period prevents flowering and allows two and even three years of vegetative growth, resulting in world-record sucrose yields. As much as 1.2% of the incident sunlight can be captured, and 0.25% converted into sucrose, so that 4.5 to 5 calories of useful product are harvested for each calorie of fossil energy input. This return for cane, maize, and other tropical grasses contrasts sharply with the return of only about 1 calorie from rice, which requires much greater inputs of water and energy. Most subsistence agriculture returns only about one for one, even with minimal input of cultural energy. Rain fed culture of cane can be profitable on certain cloudy areas like the Hamakua Coast of Hawai'i, where, despite low sunlight and low yields, three years of growth prior to harvest can be offset by low production cost.

Pineapple, a second mainstay of Hawaiian agriculture, became an important crop after the invention of the Ginacca device in the early 1900s. This permitted the mechanization of the canning operation for export of the crop. Pineapple, a terrestrial bromeliad from South America, has unique properties of water conservation associated with a metabolism that stores carbon dioxide as malic acid at night for subsequent photosynthetic activity by day. This allows stomatal pores in the leaf to remain closed for much of the day, thus greatly reducing evapotranspiration. In pineapple, moreover, the stomata on the succulent leaves are located in trenches on the underside of the leaf, covered with hairs, so that even with the stomata open, gas exchange is less than the rate for conventional leaves such as sugarcane with their stomata closed. Transpiration water loss is minimal, and total evapotranspiration is only about one-tenth that for sugarcane or a conventional grass. This conservative water use allowed rain fed

culture of pineapple on dry areas of Moloka'i and Lāna'i, where there was not sufficient water for irrigated cane production. A black vapor-barrier mulch of polyethylene plastic over perhaps half the soil surface raises the soil temperature, despite the vapor barrier, and increases the rate of soil evaporation from the pineapple planting. Originally intended for weed control, the opaque mulch increases soil temperature enough to nearly double the rate of early pineapple growth. If the pineapple trash remnant from the prior crop is left on the soil between the plant rows as insulation mulch, soil temperature is lowered, and the reduced water use allows pineapple growth under very dry conditions.

When night temperatures are high, carbon dioxide fixed in the leaf as malic acid is rapidly lost; hence, cool nights favor carbon assimilation, and thus pineapple growth. But, since the pineapple leaves are not cooled by evaporation, they overheat, despite their high heat capacity. Pineapple fruit exposed to direct sunlight may reach temperatures as high as 54°C (130°F), and is literally cooked. Although not in Hawai'i, in many other pineapple production areas the fruit must be shaded to prevent heat damage. The entire pineapple plant, with its spiral arrangement of erect leaves, has a low reflectivity to sunlight and a leaf area nearly double that of sugarcane. In Hawai'i, the plants normally remain vegetative but can be forced into flower by the application of hormones. In this way, the fruit will ripen nearly simultaneously over the entire field and can be harvested quickly. This has economic importance, since pineapple does not after-ripen and cannot be picked green and allowed to ripen for harvest, as can bananas.

Though it has excellent defenses against moisture loss, pineapple is still sensitive to moisture stress. The water stored in the succulent leaf is translocated into the fruit when needed and buffers fruit production against drought. However, the yield from irrigated pineapple fields can be 50% more than from nonirrigated fields. Drip irrigation beneath the mulch requires only small amounts of water and is particularly efficient in the establishment of the newly planted field, ensuring the high-quality translucent fruits critical for the fresh fruit market.

The production of tree crops has often been recommended as the optimal system to take advantage of the continuous growing season in the tropics. The breadfruit tree came to the Islands with the early Hawaiians, but breadfruit was not used as intensively as in other Polynesian cultures. Coconut, that ubiquitous symbol of the tropics, also came with the early settlers and served many uses within Hawaiian culture, although temperatures are too low for the commercial production of copra.

The banana, an herb rather than a true tree, was an important Hawaiian delicacy. All but two of the many different edible forms were restricted by *kapu* (taboo) to use for men only and forbidden to women. Commercial production of the Williams hybrid for the local market must compete with the imported Chiquita brand (another member of the Cavendish family). The texture and flavor of the local Apple or Brazilian banana are distinctive; it has no imported competitor.

Economic banana production requires high inputs of nitrogen and potassium fertilizers. It is confined to areas with annual rainfall above 1,270 mm (50 in), since irrigation increases production costs. Maturity at summer temperatures takes only six months, half as long as it takes at cooler winter temperatures. Bunch-weight harvest is highest in winter and lowest in late spring or early summer. Shelter from wind is absolutely essential for the shallow-rooted plant, and losses can be as great as 90% from periodic windstorms.

Coffee is another important Hawaiian crop. Coffee trees are pruned to control the production of primary and lateral branches. Flowers and fruits are normally produced in the leaf axils of lateral shoots the second season after the initial growth. Heavy fruiting in one season tends to suppress the development of subsequent laterals, with reduced potential for flowering, and trees tend to bear heavily in alternate years. In the Kona region of the Big Island, the cool, relatively dry winters are ideal for harvest, when a time of slowed growth favors bud initiation. Spring rainfall and warmth help flowering and fruit-set, while summer rains promote growth of new wood. The drier fall is best for harvest and sun-drying of the berries.

Macadamia, the world's finest dessert nut, and the principal tree crop in Hawai'i, is a member of the Proteaceae family native to the coastal rain forest of southern Queensland and northern New South Wales in Australia. The integrifolia species was first imported into Hawai'i in 1882, and selected clones now produce more than 90% of the world supply, principally on the island of Hawai'i. Macadamia is best adapted to mild, frost-free subtropical climates with more than 1,270 mm (50 in) of well-distributed annual rainfall. Trees can survive drought, but supplementary irrigation is needed for peak production in dry areas. Temperatures above 35°C (95°F) can reduce production and growth. The best conditions in Hawai'i occur between 250–600 m (700–1,800 ft) elevations. Trees are susceptible to wind damage, particularly where shallow soils restrict the rooting depth, and windbreaks are generally required. The main harvest period extends from August through January, with October and November the peak months. The mature nuts fall and must be gathered every two to three weeks during rainy weather, or monthly during dry weather, to prevent mold germination or rancidity.

Despite an intensive search for a more diversified

agriculture, only a very few additional crops have been found which meet the competition for export to the U.S. and world markets. Exotic flowers such as anthuriums and orchids are grown in the cloudy and rainy Hilo and Puna districts of Hawai'i, and proteas in the cool Maui uplands. The small-fruited solo papaya, introduced in 1911, is one tropical fruit grown for export. After being properly treated for the fruit fly, it is airfreighted to the Mainland United States. Today most of the papaya is produced in the Kapoho area of Hawai'i on porous lava, with only a minimum of ash and weathered rock as soil. The well-drained soil is essential to papaya root survival. These lands are highly productive because of the warmth at elevations up to 150 m (500 ft), adequate sunlight, relatively light winds, and a rainfall of about 2,500 mm (100 in) that is well distributed through the year. Moisture stress reduces plant growth and decreases fruit yield, so irrigation is necessary where water deficits occur during the year. In rainier areas, frequent leaf wetness requires weekly sprays to control fungus on the fruit. Most papaya is grown at low elevations, below 150 m (500 ft), since coolness at higher elevations not only reduces fruit quality but causes the tree to change sex, greatly increasing the amount of deformed, unmarketable fruit. Poor root anchorage in the rocky soil requires windbreaks every 30–45 m (100–150 ft).

Production of diversified crops for the local market in Hawai'i, and most specifically Honolulu, is plagued by the problem of small-scale pocket markets. Perhaps the largest acreage is in pasture and rangeland, which produces one-third of the beef and nearly 100% of the fresh milk used in Hawai'i.

Kikuyugrass and pangola digitgrass are the two most important pasture grasses in Hawai'i. Above 1,200 m (4,000 ft), however, growth is reduced during the cool season by temperatures below 15°C (60°F). When soil temperatures are above 15°C (60°F), dry matter production increases linearly with increase in sunlight. Thus on both counts, the dry matter production of the cooler, cloudy uplands can be less than half that of the warm lowlands. Intercropping of legumes with the grasses supplies nitrogen to increase the dry matter and also the protein content of the forage. Legumes normally cannot compete well with grasses for sunlight, although some species are more tolerant than others. With cool-season temperatures of approximately 20°C (68°F), sunlight or shading has little effect on dry matter production, but during the warm summer, with soil temperatures about 20°C (68°F), a linear decrease in dry matter occurs. Thus forage production in the cloudy uplands in winter can be less than one-half that in lowland areas.

Vegetation Zones

As discussed earlier in this chapter, the early Hawaiians attempted to describe the different kinds of forest and ground cover and to relate these vegetation types to one another. With some degree of accuracy, they also described the effects of rainfall and elevation on plant distribution and forest type (Table 7).

This zoning system has to be applied with particular topography in mind. In some areas, the kula is very wide, as it is on Maui; in other areas—at Waimānalo, Ko'olaupoko (O'ahu), for instance—it probably does not exist. Certainly the local residents would have used the terms best fitting their own environment. The Hawaiian zoning system implies long and careful observation of weather, rainfall, and forest type, and the economic products of those forests.

Listen carefully to Hawaiian songs; frequently the forest zones are mentioned. We hear *ma'ukele,* to take one example, in both Gabby Pahinui's signature, "Hi'ilawe," and in one of the recent releases by the Brothers Cazimero, one describing the Kīlauea area. And truly, on the Hilo side of Kīlauea is where the giants of the forest grow!

SUGGESTED READINGS

Battan, L. J. 1983. *Weather in your life*. San Francisco: Freeman.

Benzing, R. P. 1980. *The biology of the bromeliads*. Eureka, California: Mad River Press.

Handy, E. S. C., and Handy, E. G. 1972. *Native planters in old Hawaii: Their life, lore and environment*. Honolulu: Bishop Museum Press (Bernice P. Bishop Museum Bull. 233).

Humbert, R. P. 1968. *The growing of sugar cane*. New York: Elsevier Publishing Company.

Kirch, P. V. 1982. Transported landscapes. *Natural History* 91 (12): 32–35.

———. 1985. *Feather gods and fishhooks*. Honolulu: University of Hawaii Press.

Newman, T. S. *Hawaiian fishing and farming on the island of Hawai'i in AD 1778*. Honolulu: Dept. of Land and Natural Resources, Div. of State Parks.

Oki, D. S., and Giambelluca, T. W. 1987. DBCP, EDB, and TCP contamination of groundwater in Hawaii. *Ground Water* 25 (6):693–702.

CHAPTER 6

Past Climatic Changes

Dennis Nullet

GEOLOGICALLY SPEAKING, the Hawaiian Islands are young. Using the decay of Potassium-40 as a reference, rocks have been dated at 4.5 to 5.6 million years old on Kaua'i. Farther to the northwest, on tiny Nihoa and Necker islands, rocks have been dated at 7.5 million years and 11.3 million years old, respectively. Moving southeast from Kaua'i, the Islands become progressively younger. The island of Hawai'i is still being created through eruptions of the shield volcanoes of Mauna Loa and Kīlauea.

Long-term climate change has affected the Islands mainly through changes in global sea levels. Periods of climate warming coincided with a retreat of the earth's ice sheets and glaciers and a corresponding rise in sea level. Conversely, during cooler periods, the ice sheets expanded and sea levels dropped. Former shorelines above the present sea level can be identified by limestone deposits, laid down in coral reefs, and by shoreline formations such as sea cliffs. The Ewa plain on O'ahu is a former reef produced when sea levels were approximately 8 m (25 ft) higher, at least 38,000 years ago. The highest con-

firmed ancient reef formations have been found on Lāna'i—168 m (550 ft) above the present sea level. Lower sea levels are revealed by submerged wave-cut terraces, stream valleys that extend below sea level to these submerged terraces, and lithified sand dunes below sea level. Seismic-reflection profiling offshore of O'ahu has uncovered such a bewildering assemblage of buried terraces that it is difficult to correlate specific shorelines with global events. In part, the difficulty is compounded by a general subsidence of the Islands themselves. Geologists believe that shorelines and terraces more than 137 m (450 ft) below sea level must be the result of subsidence. Terraces as deep as 915 to 1,097 m (3,000 to 3,600 ft) have been identified near O'ahu.

Evidence for more recent climate changes comes from pollen collected in cores from Hawaiian mountain bogs. Studies based on mountain vegetation suggest that in the postglacial period, Hawai'i has experienced three principal climatic phases. The earliest period, which began at the end of the most recent ice age about 12,000 years ago (during which Mauna Kea was crowned with a permanent ice cap as evidenced by glacial moraines, erosional striations, and other glaciation features), seems to have been drier than now. The montane rain forest was restricted, and subalpine forest covered the now swampy summit of West Maui. In the second phase, the climate grew wetter, rain forest pressed back the subalpine forest, and peat deposits began to appear. Most recently, drier conditions returned to the higher elevations, and the zone of maximum rainfall moved lower on the mountains. A general lowering of the trade wind inversion could account for this shift.

These three periods reflect changing global temperatures. In Period I, glaciers retreated. Period II was the time of maximum warmth, sometimes called the Postglacial Climatic Optimum, peaking about 6,000 years ago. In the final period, temperatures decreased and most of the present-day Rocky Mountain glaciers were reestablished. It has been suggested that the last severe period of climate stress, seen in the Period III pollen statistics, corresponds with the last great migration of the Polynesians.

Recent Climate History of Hawai'i

This section presents a short discussion and analysis of the climate in Hawai'i since scientific weather observations began. Hawaiian connections with global climate change are discussed in Chapter 7.

Some of the earliest meteorological observations in Hawai'i were reported by Lt. Charles Wilkes, who, while in command of the United States Exploring Expedition, spent the winter of 1840–1841 in the Islands. Wilkes' visit to the Islands, just sixty-two years after their discovery by Captain James Cook, appears to have coincided with blustery weather. He wrote that the daytime winds "blow with great strength," though "the nights are calm and beautiful." Wilkes added a postscript to his assessment of the nocturnal weather, however. On an expedition to the summit of Mauna Loa, Wilkes' party measured 46 cm (18 in) of snow, experienced gales from the southwest gusting to 21 m/sec (47 mph), and recorded temperatures as low as -7.8 °C (18 °F). Huddling in camp near the summit, Wilkes wrote, "the howling wind . . . rendered the hours of darkness truly awful."

Wilkes reported the mean annual temperature at Honolulu to be 24.3 °C (75.8 °F), based on several years of measurements by missionaries, a figure very similar to the long-term mean of 23.9 °C (75 °F). He also listed rainfall totals of 536 mm (21.1 in) during 1837 and 1,189 mm (46.8 in) for 1838. The 1838 value is one of the highest annual rainfall totals ever recorded in Honolulu. During his stay, mean barometric pressure was 1,015 mb (29.97 in) of mercury, again approximating the long-term mean for September through April of 1,016 mb. He stated that sea-surface temperatures averaged 26.4 °C (79.5 °F), which, if accurate, would be unusually high, if they represented the open-ocean value.

In the late nineteenth century, as agricultural interests grew, more weather observations were made. Finally, shortly after the establishment of the territory's U.S. Weather Bureau Office in 1904, records called *Climatological Data* began to be published. By 1985, nearly 2,000 climatological stations (primarily for measuring rainfall) had been established and maintained at one time or another, giving Hawai'i one of the densest climate monitoring networks in the world.

To illustrate the history of the general climate during this century, weather data are graphed in Figures 6.1 and 6.2. The data are separated into climate elements related to the energy balance, radiation and temperature, and climate elements which indicate synoptic conditions, rainfall, and sea level pressure. The air temperature curve was compiled

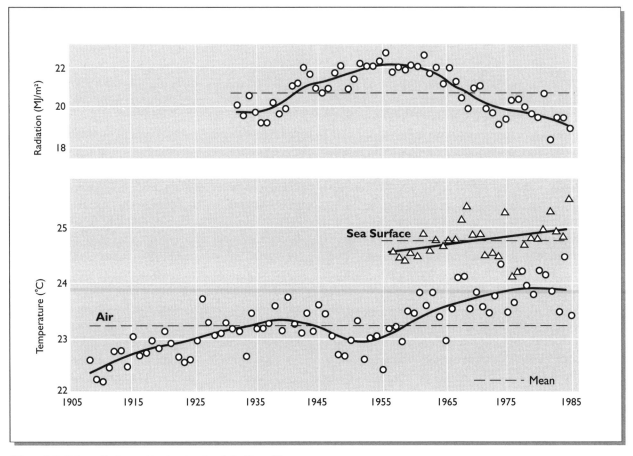

Figure 6.1 Solar radiation and temperature trends in Hawai'i

by taking the average of three windward sites: Līhu'e (Kaua'i), Hāna (Maui), and Hilo (Hawai'i). The data since 1950 represent airport records adjusted to town sites by comparing overlapping periods.

The sea surface temperature (SST) curve has been derived from weekly sea surface temperature measurements collected off Koko Head, O'ahu. Solar radiation has been measured in Honolulu since 1932, first at Hawaiian Sugar Planters' Association (HSPA's) Makiki Substation, and, since 1976, at the University of Hawaii. The rainfall and sea

level pressure data have been smoothed by calculating five-year running mean values. That is, a value plotted for a given year represents the average of that year's measurements plus the two previous and two successive years' measurements.

It has been suggested that increasing urbanization near the climate stations might hamper any attempt to identify meaningful temperature trends in the prevailing climate. It is well documented that urbanization creates local "heat islands," in which air temperatures are higher than the surrounding countryside. This is caused by an increase in absorption of solar radiation by urban surfaces and by greenhouse trapping of longwave radiation by pollutants in the air. To minimize the effect of the urban heat-island phenomenon, the air temperature record presented in this chapter was based only on records from windward stations at relatively small Līhuʻe, Hilo, and Hāna. At these sites, the urbanized area is small enough to produce only minor local warming of the air, and the heat-island phenomenon is further minimized due to mixing of surface air by the strong onshore trade winds.

It should be noted that the Honolulu temperature data, recorded near a major metropolitan area, correspond to the less-developed sites mentioned above. It should also be noted that the temperature record for Hawaiian stations corresponds well with published global temperature records.

An additional problem when compiling a Hawaiʻi temperature curve is that many of the major climate stations were moved from town sites to nearby airport sites in the 1950s. To negate the effect of this change in location, overlapping periods of record for the town and airport sites were compared for each station and the data were standardized to the original site by adding or subtracting a small correction based on the comparison. In all cases, the correction was less than $0.5\,°C$.

Climatic time series data are generally analyzed by looking for trends and cycles in the individual climatic elements and the relationships between these elements. Air temperatures rose from the beginning of the century until about 1940, declined to 1955, and then resumed the upward trend, although the year-to-year variability was greater than in the earlier periods (Figure 6.1). In support of the recent warming trend, sea surface temperatures, taken off Koko Head, Oʻahu, have risen about $0.4\,°C$ since 1955, closely matching the air temperature rise of about $0.6\,°C$ during this period. The local temperature record matches global temperature trends ex-

cept for the period of 1955–1975, when global temperatures remained fairly constant.

However, it is of interest to note that the 1961–1990 mean temperatures for the seven Hawaiian stations in Table 4 all show increases over those of the previous thirty-year period (1951–1980). For example, Honolulu's 1961–1990 mean temperature is $25.1\,°C$ ($77.2\,°F$) while the 1951–1980 value was $25.0\,°C$ ($77.0\,°F$); Lahaina $24.4\,°C$ ($76.0\,°F$) from $24.1\,°C$ ($75.3\,°F$), and Mauna Loa $7.0\,°C$ ($44.6\,°F$) from $6.7\,°C$ ($44.1\,°F$).

The cause of the temperature trend is largely a matter of speculation. Perhaps the atmospheric circulation changed or the air was warmed by greenhouse gases, such as carbon dioxide and methane. One study reported a significant easterly shift in the trade winds over Hawaiian waters between 1910 and 1940, followed by a return to more northerly winds through 1946, corresponding nicely to the temperature curve. An analysis of local winds since 1946 shows no continuation of this trend, but in the past thirty years the trades shifted slightly toward the east over the entire Pacific Ocean; such a shift would increase the southerly component of the North Equatorial Current and bring warm equatorial water into the region. In light of the importance of Mauna Loa Observatory in documenting the steady rise in atmospheric carbon dioxide, it is particularly appropriate to consider greenhouse gases, although the magnitude of the overall temperature increase since 1908 exceeds most predictions for carbon dioxide–induced warming.

In opposition to the temperature trend, measured solar radiation rose until the mid-1950s and has since declined by nearly 0.5% per year. The general shape of the radiation curve is supported by solar radiation measurements at Mauna Loa Observatory, by the hours-of-bright-sunshine measurements at Honolulu Airport, and by many agricultural solar radiation stations throughout the state. Solar radia-

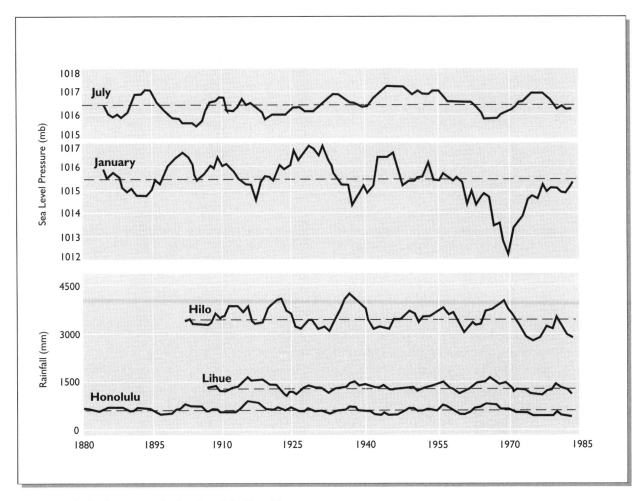

Figure 6.2 Sea level pressure and rainfall trends in Hawai'i

tion measured in the higher rainfall areas since the 1950s has generally decreased less than at the drier sites.

That the radiation trend in Hawai'i tends to oppose the temperature trend has important implications for global climatic change. A major question in climatology today is whether temperature increases due to greenhouse gases will be offset by feedback mechanisms. It has been suggested that the earth might maintain thermostasis, or constant temperature, by regulating its solar energy receipt through changes in cloudiness. In Hawai'i, as trends in atmospheric transmissivity have not been reported, the recent decrease in solar radiation at the surface is probably due to an increase in average cloudiness. This suggests that, in the Hawaiian Islands area at least, cloudiness does perhaps increase in a warmer atmosphere and thus acts as a negative feedback agent to temperature fluctuations. Similar observations have been reported for

Europe, India, and Mainland United States. Of course, it is impossible to establish a direct cause-and-effect relationship, and the inverse relation between temperature and radiation may be merely coincidental.

Unlike the energy climate elements (see Figure 6.1), the synoptic weather indicators, rainfall and atmospheric pressure, show no apparent trends in the record (Figure 6.2). A time-series analysis fails to reveal strong cyclic patterns.

The smoothed rainfall records for a windward (Hilo), leeward (Honolulu), and intermediate (Līhu'e) site generally fluctuate about the mean in phase, particularly at Līhu'e and Honolulu. This suggests common mechanisms for variation, such as the synoptic weather controls discussed in Chapter 2. Although the amplitude of rainfall fluctuations is greatest at the wet windward site, variability as a percentage of the average value is greater at the drier sites. The coefficient of variation for rainfall at Honolulu is 35% and at Hilo 21%. The mean appears stable for all three stations and indicates no long-term trends. It has been noted, however, that drought years tend to be clustered.

As with rainfall, sea level atmospheric pressure levels fluctuate evenly about a steady mean value. The variation in January pressures, subject to winter storms, pressure troughs, and migratory anticyclones, is much greater than in July, when a strong Pacific high-pressure cell is established to the north and trade winds dominate.

SUGGESTED READINGS

Gavenda, R. T. 1992. Hawaiian Quaternary paleoenvironments: A review of geological, pedological, and botanical evidence. *Pacific Science* 46 (3): 295–307.

Macdonald, G. A.; Abbott, A. T.; and Peterson, F. L. 1983. *Volcanoes in the sea: The geology of Hawaii.* Honolulu: University of Hawaii Press.

Nullet, D., and Ekern, P. C. 1988. Temperature and insolation trends in Hawaii. *Theoretical and Applied Climatology* 39:90–92.

Selling, O. H. 1948. *Studies in Hawaiian pollen statistics: Part III. On the late Quaternary history of the Hawaiian vegetation.* Honolulu: Bishop Museum Press (BPBM Special Publication 39).

CHAPTER 7

Hawaiʻi as a Site for Research in Astronomy and Climate Change

Saul Price

As was mentioned earlier in this volume, the rugged and varied topography of Hawaiʻi, with elevations ranging from sea level to 4,205 m (13,796 ft), divides the state into a variety of microclimates, each differing from the other in exposure to wind and sun, and in temperature, rainfall, and humidity. Our consideration of the role of climate in research in Hawaiʻi will be confined to a brief survey of the climate-related factors that make the high mountains outstanding sites for studies in astronomy and in the atmospheric sciences.

Astronomical Research

Within a relatively few years, Hawaiʻi has achieved universal recognition as a preeminent world center for astronomical observations and research. What has elevated it to this rank is primarily the complex of observatories straddling the summit of Mauna Kea, loftiest mountain of the Hawaiian group. Less well known, but also the site of important facilities and programs, is the so-called Science City, located at an elevation of 3,055 m (10,023 ft) on the summit of Haleakalā on the island of Maui.

The reputation of these sites within the international astronomical community derives from their exceptional optical conditions, and these in turn from the happy coincidence of a favorable climate and high mountain summits remote from urban lights and pollution. As a further advantage, both are close to the resources of a major university and readily accessible from communities and airports served by major airlines. The climatic advantages of the Mauna Kea and Haleakalā sites may be summarized as follows:

1. Moderate temperatures for the altitude. At the summit of Mauna Kea, maximum and mini-

mum temperatures average 3°C (37°F) and −4°C (25°F) respectively in winter, and about 10°C (50°F) and 0°C (32°F) in summer; on Haleakalā, they average 11°C (52°F) and 2°C (36°F) in winter and 15°C (59°F) and 5°C (41°F) in summer.

2. Infrequency of weather severe enough to prevent use of observatory facilities. Occasionally during some winters, high winds, snow, or icing over summit areas or access roads may hamper observational programs, but seldom for more than a day or two at a time.

3. A very high incidence of superior conditions for optical and infrared astronomy. According to astronomers, skies over Mauna Kea are completely clear more than 40% of the time, with 75% of the nights usable for observing. Conditions at Haleakalā are similar. The high frequency of clear days and of clean air (minimal aerosol scattering) also makes both sites ideal for observations of the solar corona and flares. Similarly, radio telescopes experience an almost complete absence of electrical interference from urban or other sources.

These unusually favorable conditions reflect in large part the influence of the trade wind inversion in restricting the influx from lower elevations of air pollution and clouds, and of the water vapor so detrimental to observations in the infrared. During the nighttime hours, the dryness and clarity of the overlying atmosphere are further enhanced by a downslope flow of air, which helps prevent residual moisture and dust from reaching the summit.

The Mauna Kea summit observatories contain some of the world's largest astronomical instruments, including the 2.24 m University of Hawaii and the 3.6 m Canada–France–Hawai'i optical telescopes, and the 3 m NASA and 3.8 m United Kingdom infrared telescopes (the latter is the largest of its kind), as well as two radio telescopes. Most of these are operated by the University of Hawaii in cooperation with international consortiums attracted to Mauna Kea by the advantages of the site. The available observing time is vastly oversubscribed, and the observatories are producing an increasing number of important discoveries in planetary, stellar, and deep-space astronomy. The Keck telescope employs a new design utilizing thirty-six 71-inch mirrors, computer-controlled to act as a single reflecting surface equivalent to a 400-in telescope in light gathering and resolving power. It is the world's largest optical telescope.

The Haleakalā summit was utilized before the Mauna Kea observatories were built. Early programs, dating back to the 1950s, included studies of the zodiacal light and of water vapor in the atmosphere of Mars. The dozen silver and white domes now scattered along the summit contain the Mees Solar Observatory, engaged in studies of the sun's corona, magnetic field, and the subsurface structure of sun spots; the Air Force's 1.6 m and 1.2 m telescopes for satellite and missile tracking and identification; the Luna Ranging Experiment (LURE), for measuring tectonic plate motion and changes in the earth's rotation via laser beams reflected from the moon; and a gamma ray telescope, operated by a consortium of U.S. and foreign universities and employing six 1.6-m mirrors.

Other solar observations in Hawai'i include solar flare monitoring at Palehua, O'ahu, as part of a global network operated by the U.S. Air Force and a coronagraph at Mauna Loa Observatory.

The Mauna Loa Observatory: Global Monitoring for Climatic Change

As part of the International Geophysical Year, the Mauna Loa Observatory (MLO) was established in 1957 at an elevation of about 3,400 m (11,200 ft) on the north-facing slope of Mauna Loa on the island of Hawai'i.

Its purpose was to monitor and establish baseline

values for certain components of the global atmosphere, including total and ambient ozone, carbon dioxide, ice nuclei concentrations, and particulates. Also included were observations of solar radiation in spectral bands, as well as the conventional weather elements, such as rainfall, temperature, precipitation, wind, humidity, sky cover, and so forth. Those original programs have since been expanded to include such other gases as methane, nitrous oxide, the chlorofluorocarbons, and carbon monoxide, as well as precipitation chemistry, lidar observations of stratospheric aerosol layers, and atmospheric turbidity.

The establishment of MLO as a global monitoring station reflected a growing awareness among scientists of many disciplines that human activities, and in particular those associated with industry, might be affecting the composition of the atmosphere. A remote, high-altitude site such as MLO offered the opportunity to obtain baseline measurements in a relatively pristine environment. For the first several years of its existence, observers overnighted at the observatory to avoid the long, difficult drive over unpaved access roads and to assure a full complement of observations. But with the development of data logging and of automation, even for instruments as complex as the Dobson spectrophotometer used for measuring total ozone, visits made only several times a week became feasible.

Carbon Dioxide, the Greenhouse Effect, and Climate Change

Of all the measurements made at MLO, it was those of carbon dioxide which first attracted worldwide attention to the observatory, and to a large degree gave rise to present interest in the so-called Carbon Dioxide Problem and greenhouse effect. What has elevated these concerns to their present importance, not only to scientists but to governments and the public at large, are the possible

consequences. Of these, the most serious is the threat of climatic change, with far-reaching social, economic, and political dislocations.

Another widespread concern is the possibility of a significant rise in sea level caused by the thermal expansion of a warming ocean and by the melting of glaciers and icecaps. By some estimates, warming associated with a doubling of CO_2 above its preindustrial values could raise sea level by 0.5 to 1 m (2 to 3 ft)—enough to cause the inland migration of many shorelines and the abandonment of or severe damage to harbors and coastal communities, installations, and facilities of all kinds. The possible impacts of an increase in atmospheric carbon dioxide, global warming, and a rising sea level in Hawai‘i will be discussed later in this section.

The greenhouse effect is already too well known to justify more than cursory mention in a volume devoted to the climate of Hawai‘i, were it not for the importance of the subject and, more particularly, the contribution of the MLO observations. Nevertheless, what follows is intended only as a brief introduction to a subject on which books and hundreds of articles have already been written. The most comprehensive analysis of every aspect of the greenhouse effect and its consequences is contained in the *Carbon Dioxide Research State-of-the-Art Report Series* recently published by the U.S. Department of Energy.

The greenhouse theory, stating that increases in the carbon dioxide content of the atmosphere could lead to a rise in global temperature, first appeared in its present form in a classic paper by Arrhenius in 1896. Perhaps the first systematic attempt to examine historical measurements of CO_2 for the existence of an upward trend in temperature was that of Callendar in 1938.

Simply put, the theory states that while the atmosphere is nearly transparent to the sun's visible and near-infrared radiation, a significant portion of the earth's return radiation is blocked or absorbed by certain of the atmosphere's gaseous components, particularly by carbon dioxide and water vapor. (The earth's radiation balance is discussed in Chapter 3.)

A beneficial consequence is that this atmospheric trapping of radiation is estimated to raise the average global temperature to its present 15°C (59°F), about 35°C (63°F) above its radiative equilibrium temperature of -20°C (-4°F), thus contributing greatly to the habitability of the earth. At the latter temperature, much of the earth's land surface would be covered by glaciers and much of the oceans by pack ice. It is difficult to visualize what life, if it had developed at all, would be like under such circumstances.

More recently, methane, nitrous oxide, carbon monoxide, and the chlorofluorocarbons have been added to the list of what are now called the greenhouse gases. Of these, methane is considered most important, because of its absorptive effects and rate of increase. What follows will be focused on CO_2, however, since it illustrates the factors involved in the greenhouse effect.

The significance of carbon dioxide in the earth's heat balance is that it absorbs terrestrial radiation strongly in several spectral bands in which water vapor absorbs weakly (see Figure 3.1). Methane and some other trace gases absorb even more strongly than CO_2 but have less effect because of their minute concentrations.

Carbon dioxide enters the atmosphere from a number of natural sources, such as the ocean, volcanic eruptions, and the burning and decay of vegetation. Large variations have occurred over time. Air bubbles from antarctic ice cores at depths reflecting glacial conditions of approximately 160,000 years ago contain CO_2 concentrations of about 200 ppm (parts per million).

Around the beginning of the industrial revolution, levels are believed to have reached about 280 ppm—a predominantly natural increase of 80 ppm in 160,000 years. They are now about 355 ppm, a further increase of 75 ppm, most of it in the past hundred years.

This recent, rapid increase is the source of present concern, since it is attributable directly to human activity—primarily to the combustion of the so-called fossil fuels, coal, oil, and natural gas by the indispensable engines of modern industry and transport, and, to a significant but lesser degree, to the destruction of tropical rain forests.

A graph of the concentrations of atmospheric CO_2 at MLO since observations began in 1957 is shown in Figure 7.1. This represents perhaps the most remarkable geophysical time series ever recorded. Individual points are monthly averages. The oscillations reflect the seasonal photosynthetic cycle of vegetation in the northern hemisphere, with CO_2 reaching its peak about February, at the end of the winter dormant period, and its minimum in autumn, at the end of the growing season when uptake of CO_2 is at its maximum.

Note that CO_2 at MLO averaged about 315 ppm when measurements began in 1957 and about 355 ppm in 1991, an increase of over 11%, or more than one ppm per year. Note, also, that the slope of the curve generally increases with time, indicating a rise in the rate of increase. Comparability of the data throughout the period of record has been ensured by the scrupulous care taken in every step of the process, from the intake of ambient air samples to the analysis of their carbon dioxide content.

On only two aspects of the carbon dioxide problem does there appear to be universal agreement. One is that the atmospheric content of CO_2 and the other greenhouse gases is, in fact, increasing, as indicated by the observations at MLO and at a worldwide GMCC (Geophysical Monitoring for Climatic Change) network. The other is that, *in the-*

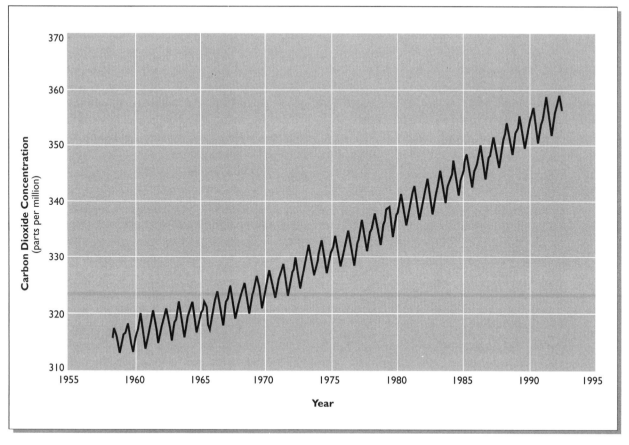

Figure 7.1 Monthly average carbon dioxide concentrations at Mauna Loa Observatory. 1958–1974. Scripps Institute of Oceanography. 1974–1991 Climate and Diagnostic Laboratory. NOAA.

ory, this increase should lead to a rise in global temperatures. But opinions differ on whether the latter will actually occur or be offset in whole or part by other changes in the atmosphere/ocean system.

Estimating the likelihood, magnitude, and effects of greenhouse warming involves many assumptions. For example, the atmosphere is but one of the reservoirs through which CO_2 moves in transiting the global carbon cycle. But too little is known about those reservoirs, and about the residence times of CO_2 within and transition rates between them, to determine whether the present increase in CO_2 will continue indefinitely or experience a significant change.

Thus, only about half the CO_2 estimated to have been put into the atmosphere by the burning of fossil fuels actually remains there. Most of the missing portion is believed to have been diffused into the ocean, which contains about sixty times as much as the atmosphere. But the continued capacity of the ocean to absorb so large a fraction of anthropogenic CO_2 is unknown.

Also uncertain is the effect of the continuing massive destruction of tropical rain forests, particularly in Southeast Asia and Brazil. Since this is destroying a major photosynthetic sink for CO_2, while at the same time creating a source through the burning and decay of the vegetation, it is generally believed to be an important contributor to the increase in atmospheric CO_2.

Using computer simulations, most scientists agree that increasing concentrations of the greenhouse gases will shift the earth's radiation balance toward global warming. Opinions differ on the extent of that warming, the rate at which it will occur, and the climatic consequences. Computer simulations are still too primitive to delineate realistically the effects even on the climate of the earth as a whole, much less on any specific part of it. The consensus is that the levels of CO_2 will be double those of preindustrial time by about the middle of the next century and increase mean global temperatures by about 1.5 °C to 4.5 °C (about 3 ° to 8 °F). Since this would occur within a time scale of decades, instead of the many millennia over which natural temperature changes of similar magnitude have occurred, there are doubts as to the ability of natural flora and fauna to adapt.

This warming would not be uniform over the earth, but would be significantly greater in polar than in tropical regions, ranging (in the northern hemisphere) from about 1.5 °C (2.7 °F) in the tropics to as much as 8 °C (14.4 °F) in polar regions. Since the tropical/polar temperature gradient is the engine that drives the atmosphere, so large a decrease in gradient could result in a major change in the general circulation of the atmosphere and in the oceanic currents.

Speculations abound. Some claim that climatic zones will advance northward several hundred kilometers, that the earth as a whole may be drier than it is now, that hurricanes may become more frequent, et cetera. But such conjectures, especially about details, ignore the complex interactions of the land-ocean-ice-atmosphere system, and the adjustments that significant change in any of these may induce in the others.

Should global warming occur, how would it affect Hawai'i? In addition to its effect on the resident population, there is concern about possible impacts on the Islands' agriculture. Most serious, however, would be injury to the Hawaiian tourist industry, mainstay of Island economy, if—for example—the climate were to become less attractive, or if Waikīkī Beach and other coastal visitor destinations were to be damaged by rising sea levels.

From what has already been said, it is evident that there are as yet no definitive answers. Hence, the following should be regarded only as possibilities. Hawai'i is an island state, far removed from the nearest continental land mass; its response to global climatic change would be modulated and moderated by the thermal inertia of the surrounding ocean. How effective this may be is indicated by reconstructions of global climate during the height of the most recent glacial period, about 18,000 years ago. These suggest that while much of Europe and North America were covered by glacial ice, ocean temperatures in the Hawaiian area were only 2 °C (3.5 °F) or so lower than they are now. This is approximately the magnitude of their present annual variation.

As the ocean warms, storm tracks would drift northward and bring Hawai'i fewer winter storms and cold fronts, with their spells of rain and cooler winds. The frequency and intensity of those storms and fronts would be further reduced by the smaller thermal contrast of polar and tropical air masses. On the other hand, tropical cyclones, many of which now remain well south of the Islands, may shift their paths northward as well, increasing their frequency in Hawai'i and—because of the warmer water—perhaps their intensity, too.

The effect of climatic change on the trade winds, so distinctive a feature of Island climate, is less certain. If, as seems possible, the Pacific high pressure system from which they come were to migrate northward, and be less frequently reinforced by strong winter anticyclones, the trades could more often give way to the light winds of Kona weather, made more sultry by offshore waters warmer than they are now. This would decrease the orographic cloud buildup and associated rainfall vital to the Islands' water balance. Combined with the lower frequency and intensity of winter storms and cold fronts, these conditions could overcome the effect of more summertime tropical cyclones and significantly reduce rainfall in the Islands.

The drier, warmer climate implied by the foregoing possibilities could have a major impact on the water balance described in Chapter 4. Evaporation would increase, while rainfall, stream flow, and aquifer recharge would all be reduced, and with them the availability of water for agriculture and for the state's resident and visitor population. This would probably necessitate more efficient use of desalination (if it were found to be economically feasible) to increase the supply of potable water. For water for crops and other nonpotable purposes, it might be necessary to rely on brackish water and treated sewage effluent. The latter is already in limited use.

Like the residents of other island and coastal regions, residents of Hawai'i have already expressed apprehension about another consequence of global warming: the rise in sea level caused by thermal expansion of the ocean and by the melting of snow cover, the permafrost, and glacial ice. First to melt might be the floating pack ice of the north polar seas. Since it already displaces its own weight of water, its melting would not appreciably alter sea level. Increased evaporation and lowered albedo over the ocean thus exposed, however, would significantly contribute to climate change.

How much might the doubling of CO_2, projected to occur by about the middle of the next century, raise sea level in Hawai'i? If, as is expected, no significant melting of the Greenland and antarctic ice sheets were to occur, it would rise probably no more than a few tenths of a meter (according to the U.S. Department of Energy's *Master Index* for the *Carbon Dioxide Research State-of-the-Art Report,* 1987). According to Dr. Klaus Wyrtki, a University of Hawaii oceanographer who has made a special study of sea level changes in the central Pacific, the rise in sea level in Honolulu over the past eighty years has averaged 1.5 mm (.06 in)/year, or 15 cm (6 in) per century.

Since 15 cm is only about one-fifth the daily range of the astronomical tide in Hawai'i (about 0.75 m) (2.5 ft), and comparable to the hydrostatic raising and lowering of sea level by migratory lows and highs, it could easily pass unnoticed. (In contrast, the rise in sea level at Hilo has averaged 3 mm (.12 in)/year, which has been attributed to sinking of the land.)

If the rise were to be as much as a meter, however, there could be significant inland encroachment by the sea. It would cover fringing reefs to a greater depth, exposing Island beaches and other low-lying coastal areas to inundation and erosion. Embankments might be needed to protect seaside hotels, airport runways, and other facilities from an increased vulnerability to damage by tides, waves, storm surges, and tsunamis. On O'ahu and elsewhere, elevation of the water table could flood low areas and reduce the volume of fresh water in underground aquifers.

Increased carbon dioxide could enhance vegetative growth through photosynthesis. Plants grown experimentally in an atmosphere enriched by CO_2 appear to increase their yield and reduce transpiration. This would presumably occur under natural conditions and could be counted as a benefit. Only a limited number and variety of plants have yet been studied, however, and other work suggests that at least in some instances such plants are lower in protein and more susceptible to insects. Research on the subject is still inconclusive.

From what has been said, it is evident that the increase in greenhouse gases and the destruction of tropical rain forests may lead to global warming and thereby to major consequences not only for climate, but for the social, economic, and political affairs of mankind. In discussing the subject, the author has attempted to point out the uncertainties and to distinguish between fact, belief, and conjecture. It is hoped that this approach will help the reader understand coming events in this important and rapidly developing field, and to assess their significance.

SUGGESTED READINGS

Callendar, G. S. 1938. The artificial production of carbon dioxide and its influence on temperature. *Quarterly Journal Royal Meteorological Society* 64:223–240.

Hansen, J., and Lebedeff, S. 1987. Global trends in measured surface air temperature. *Journal Geophysical Research* 92 (13): 345–372.

Mitchell, J. 1989. The greenhouse effect and climate change. *Review of Geophysics* 27 (1): 115–139.

Moberly, R., and MacKenzie, F. T. 1985. *Climate change and Hawaii: Significance and recommendations.* Honolulu: Hawaii Institute of Geophysics (Report HIG–85–1).

Shaw, G. E. 1979. Aerosols at Mauna Loa: Optical properties. *Journal Atmospheric Sciences* 36:862–869.

Appendix

SOURCES OF INFORMATION ON CLIMATE AND WEATHER IN HAWAI'I

Saul Price

A. Current Data (All materials listed in A are published monthly by the National Environmental Satellite and Data Service [NESDIS] through the National Climatic Data Center [NCDC]. They are available in any library that is a Federal Depository.)

1. LOCAL CLIMATOLOGICAL DATA (LCDs)

Published monthly and annually for Hilo, Honolulu, Kahului, and Līhu'e.

Monthly issues contain daily values of temperature, rainfall, wind, sunshine and other weather elements, and hourly rainfall amounts.

Annual issues contain monthly data for the current year and tables of normals, means, and extremes for the period of record.

2. CLIMATOLOGICAL DATA, HAWAII AND PACIFIC (CDs)

Published monthly and annually.

Monthly issues contain daily rainfall amounts and maximum/minimum temperatures for locations throughout the state.

Annual issues contain monthly and annual rainfall totals and departures from normal and mean monthly maximum and minimum temperatures.

3. HOURLY PRECIPITATION DATA, HAWAII AND PACIFIC (HPDs)

Published monthly and annually.

Monthly issues contain daily, hourly, and maximum short-duration rainfall amounts for the recording rain gage network.

Annual issues contain monthly and annual rainfall totals and annual maximum rainfall data by selected time categories.

All the above publications include station location maps.

4. STORM DATA

Published monthly.

Contains a brief description by states of the month's storms and unusual weather, together with deaths, injuries, and estimated property damage.

B. Historical Data (Numbers 1, 2, 3 are publications of the U.S. Weather Bureau.)

111

1. BULLETIN W

Contains monthly rainfall totals, number of rainy days, temperatures, and related data from the beginning of record.

2. CLIMATIC SUMMARY OF HAWAII, SUPPLEMENT FOR 1919–1952

3. CLIMATIC SUMMARY OF THE UNITED STATES, SUPPLEMENT FOR 1951–1960, HAWAII AND PACIFIC

Updates the previous tabulations, and adds the average frequency of days per month with rainfall amounts equal to or greater than 0.10 and 0.50 inches.

4. SOLAR RADIATION IN HAWAII, 1932–1975 (Published by the Hawaiian Sugar Planters Association 1976 [see bibliography under How].)

Monthly and annual solar radiation values and other statistics since the beginning of record. Includes station location tables and maps.

5. PAN EVAPORATION: STATE OF HAWAII, 1894–1983 (Published by Department of Land and Natural Resources, Division of Water and Land Development, Hawaii 1985 [see bibliography under Ekern and Chang].)

Monthly and annual pan evaporation values and other statistics since the beginning of record. Includes station location tables and maps.

6. CLIMATOLOGIC STATIONS IN HAWAII (Published by Department of Land and Natural Resources, Division of Water and Land Development, Hawaii Report R42, 1973.)

A catalog, arranged by station name and state key number, of all known climatologic stations in Hawai'i. Includes station location maps.

Glossary

adiabatic lapse rate: the temperature change with height inside a rising or sinking parcel of air. Adiabatic refers to temperature change without energy exchange.

advection: the transfer of a property of air, such as its sensible heat content, by the wind.

albedo: the percentage of solar radiation reflected by a surface.

anticyclone: a center of high pressure in the atmosphere characterized by counterclockwise air flow in the northern hemisphere and clockwise flow in the southern hemisphere.

Bowen ratio: the ratio of the energy at the surface used in heating the atmosphere to the amount absorbed by evaporating water.

bromelian: a New World family of plants, mostly air plants living as shrubs or trees, although they may grow in the ground or cling to rocks.

counterradiation: longwave radiation emitted by the atmosphere and received at the earth's surface.

cyclone: a center of low pressure in the atmosphere characterized by clockwise air flow in the northern hemisphere and counterclockwise flow in the southern hemisphere.

diffuse radiation: scattered or reflected solar radiation.

El Niño: a period when abnormally warm surface water persists in the equatorial central and eastern Pacific Ocean, associated with a reversal of large-scale pressure systems in the South Pacific (literal meaning "boy-child" or Christ child, referring to its appearance at Christmas).

endemic: native to an area.

energy balance: the sum of the various inputs and outputs of energy at the earth's surface.

ENSO: El Niño–Southern Oscillation, the large-scale fluctuation in the states of the atmosphere and ocean thought to be associated with unusual weather worldwide.

evapotranspiration: the loss of water to the atmosphere by evaporation and transpiration.

feral: wild.

Ghyben-Herzberg lens: a body of fresh basal groundwater in the form of a biconvex lens, floating on salt water; named for discoverers, the Dutch scientist Baden-Ghyben and the German scientist Herzberg.

global radiation: total solar radiation received on a horizontal surface.

hydrologic cycle: the movement of water between the ocean and atmosphere, atmosphere and land, and land and ocean.

infrared radiation: electromagnetic radiation having wavelengths between $0.7 \ \mu m$ and $1000 \ \mu m$.

inversion: a layer of the atmosphere in which temperature increases with altitude (as opposed to the usual temperature decrease with altitude).

Kona storm: a low-pressure system that develops in the upper atmosphere, gradually extends to lower altitudes, and may eventually appear as a surface low.

Kona weather: a period of light, variable winds in Hawai'i.

lapse rate: the rate of change of temperature with height.

latent heat: energy absorbed or released when a substance changes state.

longwave radiation: infrared radiation emitted by the earth's surface and atmosphere.

mesoscale: weather phenomena with a spatial scale from a few kilometers to a few hundred kilometers.

microclimate: the climate near the ground.

micrometer: one millionth of a meter.

mycorrhigal fungi: root fungi.

net longwave radiation: the difference between absorbed (downward) and emitted (upward) longwave radiation at the earth's surface.

net radiation: the difference between absorbed (downward) and emitted (upward) radiation of all wavelengths at the earth's surface.

orographic lifting: the forced ascent of air that occurs when wind encounters a hill or mountain.

ozone: three atoms of oxygen bonded together. The ozone layer in earth's stratosphere protects life by strongly absorbing ultraviolet radiation.

pan evaporation: evaporation from an open pan of water; used as an indication of the atmospheric demand for water from nearby vegetation, soil, or water bodies.

potential evapotranspiration: the evapotranspiration rate that would occur from a short green crop never short of water.

pyranometer: an instrument used to measure solar radiation.

radiation balance: the sum of the various inputs and outputs of radiation at the earth's surface.

recharge: water that percolates into the ground beyond the root zone, eventually entering the groundwater.

refraction: the bending of light as it passes from one medium to another. In the atmosphere refraction produces optical phenomena such as mirages and rainbows.

runoff: water that flows overland into streams.

sea breeze: onshore wind during the day resulting from the temperature difference between land and water surfaces.

sensible heat: energy stored in the motion of molecules; measured as temperature.

solar constant: the average intensity of sunlight in space at the earth's average distance from the sun; approximately 1.96 cal/cm^2/minute.

solar radiation: radiant energy emitted by the sun.

subsidence: downward movement of air in the earth's atmosphere.

subtropical high-pressure center: large centers of high pressure usually present near $30°$ Latitude North and South of the equator over the oceans.

synoptic scale: weather phenomena with a spatial scale from a few hundred to a few thousand kilometers.

terrestrial radiation: infrared radiation emitted by the earth's surface and atmosphere.

trade winds: the persistent easterly winds characteristic of the tropics.

trichomes: hair.

troposphere: the layer of the atmosphere nearest the earth's surface in which the air temperature usually decreases with height.

ultraviolet radiation: electromagnetic radiation having wavelengths between 0.01 μm and 0.40 μm.

visible light: electromagnetic radiation that the human eye can see, including all wavelengths between about 0.4 and 0.7 micrometers.

vog: volcanic smoke and haze (combination of "volcanic" and "fog").

water balance: the sum of the various inputs and outputs of water at the earth's surface.

Bibliography

American Meteorological Society. 1951. On the rainfall of Hawaii: A group of contributions. *Meteorological Monographs* 1 (3): 1–55.

Arrhenius, S. 1896. On the influence of the carbonic acid in the air upon the temperature of the ground. *Philosophy Magazine* 21, 237–276.

Beaumont, J. H., and Fukunaga, E. T. 1958. Factors affecting the growth and yield of coffee in Kona, Hawaii. *Hawaii Agricultural Dept. Station Bulletin* 113: 39 pp.

Belshe, J. C. 1975. *Terrestrial ecosystems in the Hawaii region.* Honolulu: Hawaii Water Resources Regional Study.

Benzing, R. P. 1980. *The biology of the bromeliads.* Eureka, California: Mad River Press.

Best, R. 1962. Production factors in the tropics. *Netherlands Journal Agricultural Science* 10 (5): 347–353.

Bienroth, F. H.; Ikawa, H.; and Uehara, G. 1979. Classification of the soil series of Hawaii in four systems. *HAES Misc. Pub. 166 (BSP Tech. Rep. 2):* 56 pp.

Blumenstock, D. I., and Price, S. 1967. "Climates of the states: Hawaii." In *Climatography of the United States No. 60–51.* U.S. Department of Commerce.

Britten, E. J. 1959. Volcano ranching. *Journal Range Management* 12 (6): 303–306.

———. 1962. Hawaii as a natural laboratory. *Pacific Science* 16 (2): 160–169.

Brodie, H. W. 1964. Instruments for measuring solar radiation: Research and evaluation by the Hawaiian sugar industry 1928–1962. *Hawaiian Planter's Record* 57:159–197.

———. 1965. The wig-wag. *Solar Energy* 9:27–31.

Brown, R. H. 1985. Growth of C3 and C4 grasses under low nitrogen levels. *Crop Science* 25:954–957.

Callendar, G. S. 1938. The artificial production of carbon dioxide and its influence on temperature. *Quarterly Journal Royal Meteorological Society* 64:223–240.

Campbell, R. B.; Chang, J. H.; and Cox, D. C. 1960. Evapotranspiration in Hawaii as measured by in-field lysimeters in relation to climate. *Proceedings International Society Sugar Cane Technology* 10:645–73.

Carlquist, S. 1981. Chance dispersal. *American Scientist* 69: 509–516.

Chang, J. H. 1959. An evaluation of the 1948 Thornthwaite Classification. *Annals Association American Geographers* 49: 24–30.

———. 1961. Microclimate of sugar cane. *Hawaiian Planter's Record* 56:195–223.

———. 1963. The role of climatology in the Hawaiian sugar cane industry: An example of applied agricultural climatology in the tropics. *Pacific Science* 17:379–397.

Chang, J. H.; Campbell, R. B.; Brodie, H. W.; and Baver, L. D. 1967. Evapotranspiration research at the HSPA experiment station. *Proceedings International Society Sugar Cane Technology.*

Charnell, R. L. 1967. Long-wave radiation near the Hawaiian Islands. *Journal Geophysical Research* 72 (2): 489–495.

Chen, Y. L., and Schroeder, T. A. 1986. The relationship among local winds, synoptic-scale flow and precipitation at Hilo during HAMEL. *International Conference on Monsoon and Mesoscale Meteorology (Preprints):* 191–195. Taipei: American Meteorological Society.

Cheng, E. D. H., and Lan, L. S. 1973. *Some statistical analyses of Hawaiian rainfall.* Honolulu: Water Resources Research Center, University of Hawaii (Technical Report No. 72).

Chiu, A. N. L.; Escalante, L. E.; Mitchell, J. K.; Perry,

D. C.; Schroeder, T. A.; and Walton, T. 1983. *Hurricane Iwa, Hawaii: November 23, 1982.* Washington, D.C.: National Research Council, 129 pp.

Clements, H. F. 1980. *Sugarcane crop logging and crop control.* Honolulu: University of Hawaii Press, 520 pp.

Culliney, J. L. 1988. *Islands in a far sea: Nature and man in Hawaii.* San Francisco: Sierra Club Books, pp. 313–352.

de Brain, H. A. R. 1983. "Evapotranspiration in humid tropical regions." In *Hydrology of humid tropical regions,* ed. R. Keller, 299–311. International Association Hydrological Science Pub. No. 140.

Department of Geography, University of Hawaii. 1973. *Atlas of Hawaii.* Honolulu: University of Hawaii Press.

Dorman, C. E., and Bourke, R. H. 1979. Precipitation over the Pacific Ocean: 30°S to 60°N. *Monthly Weather Review* 107:896–910.

Drummond, A. J., and Angstrom, A. K. 1967. Solar radiation measurements on Mauna Loa, Hawaii. *Solar Energy* 11:1–9.

Ekern, P. C. 1959. Evapotranspiration patterns under trade wind weather regime on central Oahu, Hawaii. *Agronomy Abstracts* 6:4–5.

———. 1965a. Evapotranspiration of pineapple in Hawaii. *Plant Physiology* 40:736–739.

———. 1965b. The fraction of sunlight retained as net radiation in Hawaii. *Journal Geophysical Research* 70 (4): 785–793.

———. 1965c. Disposition of net radiation by a free water surface in Hawaii. *Journal Geophysical Research* 70:795–800.

———. 1978. Variation in sunlight induced by topography under the trade wind regime on Oahu, Hawaii. *Proceedings: Conference on Climate and Energy.* Asheville, North Carolina: American Meteorological Society.

———. 1983. *Measured evapotranspiration in high rainfall areas: Leeward Koolau Range, Hawaii.* Honolulu: Water Resources Research Center, University of Hawaii (Technical Report No. 156).

Ekern, P. C., and Becker, R. J. 1982. *Project ahupua'a: Solar meteorological field measurements on the island of Hawai'i, summer 1978 (5: Southern flank of Mauna Loa).* Honolulu: University of Hawaii, Meteorology Department (Report UHMET 79-08).

Ekern, P. C., and Chang, J. H. 1985. *Pan Evaporation, State of Hawaii: 1894–1983.* Honolulu: Water Resources Research Center. University of Hawaii (Report R74).

Ekern, P. C., and Worthley, L. E. 1968. *Annotated bibliography of publications and papers relevant to Hawaiian weather.*

Honolulu: Hawaii Institute of Geophysics (Report HIG-68–11).

Elliott, W. P., and Reed, R. K. 1984. A climatological estimate of precipitation for the world ocean. *Journal Applied Meteorology* 23:434–439.

Ellis, H. T., and Pueschel R. F. 1971. Solar radiation: Absence of air pollution trends at Mauna Loa. *Science* 172:845–846.

Eriksen, F. I., and Whitney, A. S. 1982. Growth of tropical forage legumes. *Agronomy Journal* 74:703–709.

Feldwisch, W. F. 1941. "Supplementary climatic notes for the Hawaiian Islands." In *Climate and man: Yearbook of agriculture,* 1216–1221.

Garrett, A. J. 1980. Orographic cloud over the eastern slopes of Mauna Loa Volcano, Hawaii, related to insolation and wind. *Monthly Weather Review* 108:931–941.

Gavenda, R. T. 1992. Hawaiian Quaternary paleoenvironments: A review of geological, pedological and botanical evidence. *Pacific Science* 46 (3): 295–307.

Giambelluca, T. W. 1983. Water balance of the Pearl Harbour Honolulu Basin, Hawaii: 1946–1975. *Technical Report No. 151: Water Resources Research Center.* University of Hawaii.

———. 1986. Land use effects on the water balance of a tropical island. *National Geographic Research* 2:125–151.

Giambelluca, T. W.; Lau, L. S.; Fok, Y. S.; and Schroeder, T. A. 1984. *Rainfall frequency study for Oahu.* Honolulu: State of Hawaii, Department of Land and Natural Resources, Division of Water and Land Development (Report R73).

Giambelluca, T. W.; McKenna, D.; and Ekern, P. C. 1992. An automated recording atmometer: 1. Calibration and testing. *Journal of Agricultural and Forest Meteorology* 62:109–125.

Giambelluca, T. W., and Nullet, D. 1991. Influence of the trade-wind inversion on the climate of a leeward mountain slope in Hawaii. *Climate Research* 1 (3): 207–216.

———. 1992a. An automated recording atmometer: 2. Evaporation measurement on a high elevation transect in Hawaii. *Journal of Agricultural and Forest Meteorology* 62:127–138.

———. 1992b. Evaporation at high elevations in Hawaii. *Journal of Hydrology* 136:219–235.

Giambelluca, T. W.; Nullet D; and Schroeder, T. A. 1986. *Rainfall atlas of Hawaii.* Honolulu: Water Resources Research Center, University of Hawaii (Report No. R76).

Hahn, S. K. 1975. Sweet potatoes productivity. *Symposium on ecophysiology of tropical crops.* Academic Press.

Hansen, J., and Lebedeff, S. 1987. Global trends in measured surface air temperature. *Journal Geophysical Research* 92 (13): 345–372.

Harris, D. R. 1972. Origins of agriculture in the tropics. *American Scientist* 60:180–193.

Hawaii State Water Commission. 1979. *Hawaii's water resources: Directions for the future.* A report to the Governor of the State of Hawaii.

Hawaii Water Authority. 1959. *Water Resources in Hawaii.* Territory of Hawaii.

Heichel, G. H. 1976. Agricultural production and energy resources. *American Scientist* 64:64–72.

Helvey, J. D., and Patric, J. H. 1983. Sampling accuracy of pit vs. standard rain gages on the Femour Experimental Forest. *Water Resources Bulletin* 19:87–89.

Henry, A. J. 1925. Hawaiian rainfall. *Monthly Weather Review* 53:10–14.

Hoerl, A. E., and Kennard, R. W. 1970. Ridge regression: Biased estimation for nonorthogonal problems. *Telemetrics* 12:55–67.

How, K. T. S. 1978. *Solar radiation in Hawaii: 1932–75.* Honolulu: Hawaiian Sugar Planters Association for Division Water and Land Development, Dept. Land and Natural Resources.

Humbert, R. P. 1968. *The growing of sugar cane.* New York: Elsevier Publishing Company.

Jackson, M. L., et al. 1971. Geomorpheal relationships: Soils in Hawaiian isles. *SSSAP* 35:515–525.

Janzen, D. H. 1973. Tropical agroecosystems. *Science* 182: 1212–1219.

Jones, C. A. 1980. A review of evapotranspiration studies in irrigated sugar cane in Hawaii. *Hawaiian Planter's Record* 59:195–214.

Jones, S. B. 1939. The weather element in the Hawaiian climate. *Annals Association American Geographers* 29 (1): 29–57.

Jones, S. B., and Bellaire, R. 1937. The classification of Hawaiian climates: A comparison of the Koppen and Thornthwaite systems. *Geographical Review* 27:112–119.

Jong, K. G., et al. 1982. Solar radiation and maize. *Crop Science* 22:13–18.

Juvik, J. O., and Ekern, P. C. 1978. *A climatology of mountain fog on Mauna Loa, Hawaiian Islands.* Honolulu: Water Resources Research Center, University of Hawaii (Technical Rep. No. 118).

Juvik, J. O., and Perreira, D. J. 1974. Fog interception on Mauna Loa, Hawaii. *Proceedings Conference, Association American Geographers* 6:22–25.

Juvik, J. 0.; Singleton, D. C.; and Clarke, G. G. 1978. "Climate and water balance on the island of Hawaii." In *Mauna Loa Observatory,* ed. J. Miller, 129–139. Twentieth Anniversary Report, U.S. Dept. Commerce, NOAA Environmental Research Laboratory.

Kamakau, S. M. 1976. *The works of the people of old.* Honolulu: Bishop Museum Press.

Kirch, P. V. 1985. *Feather gods and fishhooks.* Honolulu: University of Hawaii Press.

Kurtyka, J. C. 1953. *Precipitation measurements study.* Urbana: Illinois State Water Survey (Report of Investigation 20).

Landsberg, H. 1951. Statistical investigations into the climatology of rainfall on Oahu. *Meteorological Monographs* 1 (3): 7–23.

Lanner, R. M. 1966. Phenology and growth habits of pines in Hawai'i. *U.S. Forest Service Research Paper PSW-29.*

Larson, L. W., and Peck, E. L. 1974. Accuracy of precipitation measurements for hydrological modeling. *Water Resources Research:* 857–863.

Leopold, L. B. 1948. The interaction of trade wind and sea breeze. *Journal Meteorology* 6 (5): 312–320.

Loveridge, E. F. 1924. Diurnal variations of precipitation at Honolulu, Hawaii. *Monthly Weather Review* 52:584–585.

Lyons, S. W. 1982. Empirical orthogonal function analysis of Hawaiian rainfall. *Journal Applied Meteorology* 21:1713–1729.

Malkus, J. S. 1958. "On the structure of the trade wind moist layer." *Papers in Physical Oceanography and Meteorology* 13 (2): 1–47.

Malo, D. 1980. *Hawaiian antiquities.* Honolulu: Bishop Museum Press.

McCall, W. W. 1975. Soil classification in Hawaii. V.H. CES Circular 476.

Meisner, B. N. 1976. *A study of Hawaiian and Line Islands rainfall.* Honolulu: Dept. Meteorology, University of Hawaii (U.H. Met. 76-04).

———. 1978. Hawaiian rainfall climatography. Ph.D. dissertation, University of Hawaii, Honolulu.

———. 1979. Ridge regression: Time extrapolation applied to Hawaiian rainfall normals. *Journal Applied Meteorology* 18:904–912.

Meisner, B. N., and Schroeder, T. A. 1982. *Median rainfall: State of Hawaii.* Honolulu: Dept. Land and Natural Resources, Division of Water and Land Development (Circular 88).

Mendonca, B. G. 1969. Local wind circulations on the slope of Mauna Loa. *Journal Applied Meteorology* 8:533–541.

Mendonca, B. G., and Iwaoka, W. T. 1969. The trade wind inversion at the slopes of Mauna Loa, Hawai'i. *Journal Applied Meteorology* 8:213–219.

Mink, J. F. 1960. Distribution pattern of rainfall in the leeward Koolau mountains, Oahu, Hawaii. *Journal Geophysical Research* 65:2869–2876.

———. 1962. Rainfall and runoff in the leeward Koolau Mountains, Oahu, Hawaii. *Pacific Science* 16 (2): 147–159.

Mitchell, J. 1989. The "Greenhouse effect" and "climate change." *Review of Geophysics* 27 (1): 115–139.

Moberly, R., and MacKenzie, F. T. 1985. *Climate change and Hawaii: Significance and recommendations.* Honolulu: Hawaii Institute of Geophysics (Report HIG-85-1).

Mooney, H. A., et al. The study of physiological ecology of tropical plants. *Bio Science* 30 (1): 22–28.

Morgan, J. R. 1983. *Hawaii: A geography. In Westview Geographies of the United States.* Ingolf Vogeler Series Editor. Boulder, Colorado: Westwood Press.

Mott, G. O., and Popenoe, H. L. 1977. Tropical grasslands. Ecolophysiology of tropical crops.

Mueller-Dombois, D. 1966. "Climate." *Chap. IV* in *Atlas for Bioecology Studies in Hawaii Volcanoes National Park.* U.S. National Park Service.

———. 1985. 'Ohi'a dieback in Hawai'i: 1984 synthesis and evaluation. *Pacific Science* 39:150–170.

Mueller-Dombois, D., and Krajina, V. G. 1968. East flank vegetables. *Proc. Recent Advances Tropical Ecology.* International Society Tropical Ecology: 508–520.

Noguchi, Y. 1979. Deformation of trees in Hawaii and its relation to wind. *Journal Ecology* 67 (2): 611–628.

Nullet, D. 1987. Energy sources for evaporation on tropical islands. *Physical Geography* 8 (1): 36–45.

Nullet, D., and Ekern, P. C. 1988a. Modeling clear day insolation in Hawaii. *Solar Energy* 40 (3): 187–189.

———. 1988b. Temperature and insolation trends in Hawaii. *Theoretical and Applied Climatology* 39:90–92.

Nullet, D., and Giambelluca, T. W. 1990. Winter evaporation on a mountain slope, Hawaii. *Journal of Hydrology* 112:257–265.

———. 1992. Radiation climatology through the trade-wind inversion. *Physical Geography* 13 (1): 66–80.

Nullet, D., and McGranaghan, M. 1988. Rainfall enhancement over the Hawaiian Islands. *Journal Climate* 1 (8): 837–839.

Oki, D. S., and Giambelluca, T. W. 1985. *Subsurface water and soil quality data base for State of Hawaii.* Honolulu: University of Hawaii, Water Resources Research Center (Special Report 7:85).

———. 1987. DBCP, EDB, and TCP contamination of groundwater in Hawaii. *Ground Water* 25 (6): 693–702.

Price, S. 1971. "Some aspects of the rainfall climate of the Hawaiian Islands." In *Hydrologic systems in Hawaii.* Honolulu: United States-Japan Bilateral Seminar in Hydrology.

———. 1983. "Climate." In *Atlas of Hawaii,* 2nd edition 53–60. Honolulu: University of Hawaii Press.

Price, S., and Pales, J. C. 1959. The Mauna Loa high-altitude observatory. *Monthly Weather Review* 87:1–14.

———. 1963. Mauna Loa Observatory: The first five years. *Monthly Weather Review* 91:665–680.

Price, S., and Sasaki, R. I. 1963. Some tornadoes, waterspouts and other funnel clouds of Hawaii. *Monthly Weather Review* 91 (4): 175–190.

Project Shower. 1957. (A collective set of fifteen papers) *Tellus* 9:471–590.

Pukui, Mary K., et al. 1981. *Place names of Hawaii.* Honolulu: University of Hawaii Press.

Ramage, C. S. 1962. The subtropical cyclone. *Journal Geophysical Research* 67:1401–1411.

———. 1978. Effect of Hawaiian Islands on trade winds. *Conference on Climate and Energy.* Asheville, N.C.: American Meteorological Society.

———. 1979. Prospecting for meteorological energy in Hawaii. *Bulletin American Meteorogical Society* 60:430–438.

———. 1986. El Niño. *Scientific American* 254 (6): 76–83.

Reed, R. K. 1980. Comparison of ocean and island rainfall in the tropical North Pacific. *Journal Applied Meteorology* 19 (7): 877–878.

Ridgley, M. A., and Giambelluca, T. W. 1991. Drought, groundwater management and land use planning: The case of central Oahu, Hawaii. *Applied Geography* 11:289–307.

———. 1992. Linking water-balance simulation and multiobjective programming: Land-use plan design in Hawaii. *Environment and Planning Bulletin* 19:317–336.

Riehl, H. 1949. Some aspects of Hawaiian rainfall. *Bulletin American Meteorological Society* 30:176–187.

Robinson, F. E.; Campbell, R. B.; and Chang, J. H. 1963. Assessing the utility of pan evaporation for controlling irrigation of sugar cane in Hawaii. *Agronomy Journal* 55 (5): 444–446.

Riley, T. J. 1973. Wet and dry in a Hawaiian valley: The

archeology of an agricultural system. Ph.D. dissertation, Dept. Anthropology, University of Hawaii (247 pp.).

Schooley, A. H. 1969. Radiation measurements at sea. *Journal Geophysical Research* 74:958–961.

Schroeder, T. A. 1977a. Hawaiian waterspouts and tornadoes. *Monthly Weather Review* 105:1163–1170.

———. 1977b. Meteorological aspects of an Oahu flood. *Monthly Weather Review* 105:458–468.

———. 1977c. Severe downslope winds in Oahu. *Tenth Conference Severe Local Storms*. Omaha, Nebraska: American Meteorological Society, 373–375.

———. 1981a. A revised precipitation climatology for the Hawaiian Islands. *Fourth Conference Hydrometeorology*. Reno, Nevada: American Meteorological Society, 73–75.

———. 1981b. Characteristics of local winds in northwest Hawaii. *Journal Applied Meteorology* 20:874–881.

———. 1981c. Drainage winds related to prevailing winds and topography. *Second Conference Mountain Meteorology*. Steamboat Springs, Colorado: American Meteorological Society, 233–237.

———. 1981d. Torrential rains on the Island of Hawaii: 1979–1980. *Fourth Conference Hydrometeorology*. Reno, Nevada: American Meteorological Society, 212–214.

Schroeder, T. A., and Hori, A. M. 1980. *Wind energy resource atlas: Hawaii and Pacific Island regions*. Richland, Washington. Battelle Pacific Northwest Laboratories (PNL–3195WERA–11).

Sellers, W. D. 1965. *Physical climatology*. Chicago: University of Chicago Press.

Shaw, G. E. 1979. Aerosols at Mauna Loa: Optical properties. *Journal Atmospheric Sciences* 36:862–869.

———. 1980. Transport of Asian desert aerosol to the Hawaiian Islands. *Journal Applied Meteorology* 19:1254–1259.

Shaw, S. L. 1981. *A history of tropical cyclones in the central North Pacific and the Hawaiian Islands: 1832–1979*. Washington, D.C.: U.S. Dept. Commerce, NOAA, National Weather Service, 137 pp.

Shih, S. F., and Snyder, G. H. 1985. LAI and ET of tars. *Agronomy Journal* 77:554–556.

Simpson, R. H. 1952. Evaluation of the Kona storm: A subtropical cyclone. *Journal Meteorology* 9 (1): 24–35.

Solot, S. B. 1900. *Further studies in Hawaiian precipitation*. Washington, D.C.: U.S. Weather Bureau Research Paper No. 32.

Stidd, C. K., and Leopold, L. B. 1951. The geographic distribution of average monthly rainfall. *Hawaii Meteorological Monographs* 1 (3): 24–33.

Takasaki, K. J.; Hirashima, G. T.; and Labke, E. R. 1969. *Water resources of windward Oahu*. Washington, D.C.: U.S. Geological Survey Water Supply Paper 1894.

Taliaferro, W. J. 1958. *Kona rainfall*. Honolulu: Hawaii Water Authority.

———. 1959. *Rainfall of the Hawaiian Islands*. Honolulu: Hawaii Water Authority.

Taylor, G. E. 1984. Hawaiian winter rainfall and its relation to the Southern Oscillation. *Monthly Weather Review* 112: 1613–1619.

Thompson, T. M., and Cox, S. K. 1982. Subtropical climatology of direct beam solar radiation. *Journal Applied Meteorology* 21:334–338.

Thornthwaite, C. W. 1948. An approach toward a rational classification of climate. *Geographical Review* 38:55–94.

Thornthwaite, C. W., and Mather, J. R. 1955. *The water balance*. Centerton, New Jersey: Publications in Climatology, Laboratory of Climatology.

Triyillo, E. E. 1965. Phytophthora blight of taro. *Phytopath* 55 (2): 183–188.

U.S. Department of Energy. 1987. *Master index for the carbon dioxide research state of the art report series*. Washington, D.C.

Warm Rain Project. 1967. (A collective set of eleven papers). *Tellus* 19:347–461.

Whitney, S. 1984. Growth of Kikuyugrass. *Agronomy Journal* 66:281–287.

Worthley, L. E. 1967. *Synoptic climatology of Hawaii*. Honolulu: Hawaiian Institute Geophysics (Final Report, Contract No. CWb 11373, 1–40).

Yee, W., et al. 1970. *Papayas in Hawaii*. Honolulu: University of Hawaii CES circular 436.

Yeh, T. C.; Wallen, C. C.; and Carsen, J. E. 1951. "A study of rainfall over Oahu." In *On the rainfall of Hawaii*. *Meteorological Monographs* 1 (3): 34–46.

Yoshihara, T., and Ekern, P. C. 1977. *Solar radiation measurements in Hawaii*. Honolulu: The Hawaii Natural Energy Institute, University of Hawaii.

———. 1978. *Assessment of the potential of solar energy in Hawaii*. Honolulu: The Hawaii Natural Energy Institute, University of Hawaii.

List of Contributors

MARIE SANDERSON is a member of the Geography Department and the Director of a water research group called The Water Network at the University of Waterloo, Ontario, Canada. Collaboration on this book began when she was a visiting professor in the Department of Geography, University of Hawaii at Manoa.

PAUL EKERN recently retired from the Water Resources Research Center at the University of Hawaii, where for many years he conducted climate and water research in the Islands, specializing in radiation and evapotranspiration.

TOM GIAMBELLUCA is an associate professor in the Department of Geography at the University of Hawaii at Manoa. His research interests are primarily in climatology, with a specialty in water balance and rainfall in the Islands.

DENNIS NULLET is currently a professor of climatology in the Department of Geography at the University of Hawaii at Hilo. He received his Ph.D. in geography at the University of Hawaii. His primary area of research is Hawaiian climate.

SAUL PRICE recently retired from the National Weather Service, Pacific Region, in Honolulu. He has written extensively on Mauna Loa Observatory and on the climate of the Islands, including articles in *The Atlas of Hawaii* and, with David Blumenstock, in the *Climates of the States* series.

THOMAS SCHROEDER is a mesometeorologist with the Department of Meteorology at the University of Hawaii. He has done extensive research on local weather patterns and severe storms in Hawai'i and has taught introductory courses on the weather and climate of Hawai'i since 1974.

Index